# THE BATTLE OF SPRING HILL

# THE LOCHLAINN SEABROOK COLLECTION

## AMERICAN CIVIL WAR
Abraham Lincoln Was a Liberal, Jefferson Davis Was a Conservative: The Missing Key to Understanding the American Civil War
Confederacy 101: Amazing Facts You Never Knew About America's Oldest Political Tradition
Confederate Blood and Treasure: An Interview With Lochlainn Seabrook
Everything You Were Taught About African-Americans and the Civil War is Wrong, Ask a Southerner!
Everything You Were Taught About the Civil War is Wrong, Ask a Southerner!
Give This Book to a Yankee! A Southern Guide to the Civil War For Northerners
Lincoln's War: The Real Cause, the Real Winner, the Real Loser
The Great Yankee Coverup: What the North Doesn't Want You to Know About Lincoln's War!
The Ultimate Civil War Quiz Book: How Much Do You Really Know About America's Most Misunderstood Conflict?
Women in Gray: A Tribute to the Ladies Who Supported the Southern Confederacy

## CONFEDERATE MONUMENTS
Confederate Monuments: Why Every American Should Honor Confederate Soldiers and Their Memorials

## CONFEDERATE FLAG
Confederate Flag Facts: What Every American Should Know About Dixie's Southern Cross

## SECESSION
All We Ask Is To Be Let Alone: The Southern Secession Fact Book

## SLAVERY
Everything You Were Taught About American Slavery is Wrong, Ask a Southerner!
Slavery 101: Amazing Facts You Never Knew About America's "Peculiar Institution"

## CHILDREN
Honest Jeff and Dishonest Abe: A Southern Children's Guide to the Civil War
Saddle, Sword, and Gun: A Biography of Nathan Bedford Forrest For Teens

## NATHAN BEDFORD FORREST
A Rebel Born: A Defense of Nathan Bedford Forrest - Confederate General, American Legend (winner of the 2011 Jefferson Davis Historical Gold Medal)
A Rebel Born: The Screenplay (film about N.B. Forrest)
Forrest! 99 Reasons to Love Nathan Bedford Forrest
Give 'Em Hell Boys! The Complete Military Correspondence of Nathan Bedford Forrest
Nathan Bedford Forrest and African-Americans: Yankee Myth, Confederate Fact
Nathan Bedford Forrest and the Battle of Fort Pillow: Yankee Myth, Confederate Fact
Nathan Bedford Forrest and the Ku Klux Klan: Yankee Myth, Confederate Fact
Nathan Bedford Forrest: Southern Hero, American Patriot - Honoring a Confederate Icon and the Old South
Saddle, Sword, and Gun: A Biography of Nathan Bedford Forrest For Teens
The God of War: Nathan Bedford Forrest As He Was Seen By His Contemporaries
The Quotable Nathan Bedford Forrest: Selections From the Writings and Speeches of the Confederacy's Most Brilliant Cavalryman

## QUOTABLE SERIES
The Alexander H. Stephens Reader: Excerpts From the Works of a Confederate Founding Father
The Quotable Alexander H. Stephens: Selections From the Writings and Speeches of the Confederacy's First Vice President
The Quotable Jefferson Davis: Selections From the Writings and Speeches of the Confederacy's First President
The Quotable Nathan Bedford Forrest: Selections From the Writings and Speeches of the Confederacy's Most Brilliant Cavalryman
The Quotable Robert E. Lee: Selections From the Writings and Speeches of the South's Most Beloved Civil War General
The Quotable Stonewall Jackson: Selections From the Writings and Speeches of the South's Most Famous General
The Unquotable Abraham Lincoln: The President's Quotes They Don't Want You To Know!

CONSTITUTIONAL HISTORY
The Articles of Confederation Explained: A Clause-by-Clause Study of America's First Constitution
The Constitution of the Confederate States of America Explained: A Clause-by-Clause Study of the South's Magna Carta

VICTORIAN CONFEDERATE LITERATURE
Rise Up and Call Them Blessed: Victorian Tributes to the Confederate Soldier, 1861-1901
The God of War: Nathan Bedford Forrest As He Was Seen By His Contemporaries
The Old Rebel: Robert E. Lee As He Was Seen By His Contemporaries
Victorian Confederate Poetry: The Southern Cause in Verse, 1861-1901

ABRAHAM LINCOLN
Abraham Lincoln: The Southern View - Demythologizing America's Sixteenth President
Lincolnology: The Real Abraham Lincoln Revealed in His Own Words - A Study of Lincoln's Suppressed, Misinterpreted, and Forgotten Writings and Speeches
The Great Impersonator! 99 Reasons to Dislike Abraham Lincoln
The Unholy Crusade: Lincoln's Legacy of Destruction in the American South
The Unquotable Abraham Lincoln: The President's Quotes They Don't Want You To Know!

CIVIL WAR BATTLES
Encyclopedia of the Battle of Franklin - A Comprehensive Guide to the Conflict that Changed the Civil War
Nathan Bedford Forrest and the Battle of Fort Pillow: Yankee Myth, Confederate Fact
The Battle of Spring Hill: Recollections of Confederate and Union Soldiers

PARANORMAL
Carnton Plantation Ghost Stories: True Tales of the Unexplained from Tennessee's Most Haunted Civil War House!
UFOs and Aliens: The Complete Guidebook

FAMILY HISTORIES
The Blakeneys: An Etymological, Ethnological, and Genealogical Study - Uncovering the Mysterious Origins of the Blakeney Family and Name
The Caudills: An Etymological, Ethnological, and Genealogical Study - Exploring the Name and National Origins of a European-American Family
The McGavocks of Carnton Plantation: A Southern History - Celebrating One of Dixie's Most Noble Confederate Families and Their Tennessee Home

MIND, BODY, SPIRIT
Autobiography of a Non-Yogi: A Scientist's Journey From Hinduism to Christianity (Dr. Amitava Dasgupta, with Lochlainn Seabrook)
Britannia Rules: Goddess-Worship in Ancient Anglo-Celtic Society - An Academic Look at the United Kingdom's Matricentric Spiritual Past
Christ Is All and In All: Rediscovering Your Divine Nature and the Kingdom Within
Christmas Before Christianity: How the Birthday of the "Sun" Became the Birthday of the "Son"
Jesus and the Gospel of Q: Christ's Pre-Christian Teachings As Recorded in the New Testament
Jesus and the Law of Attraction: The Bible-Based Guide to Creating Perfect Health, Wealth, and Happiness Following Christ's Simple Formula
Seabrook's Bible Dictionary of Traditional and Mystical Christian Doctrines
The Bible and the Law of Attraction: 99 Teachings of Jesus, the Apostles, and the Prophets
The Book of Kelle: An Introduction to Goddess-Worship and the Great Celtic Mother-Goddess Kelle, Original Blessed Lady of Ireland
The Goddess Dictionary of Words and Phrases: Introducing a New Core Vocabulary for the Women's Spirituality Movement
The Way of Holiness: The Story of Religion and Myth From the Cave Bear Cult to Christianity

WOMEN
Aphrodite's Trade: The Hidden History of Prostitution Unveiled
Princess Diana: Modern Day Moon-Goddess - A Psychoanalytical and Mythological Look at Diana Spencer's Life, Marriage, and Death (with Dr. Jane Goldberg)
Women in Gray: A Tribute to the Ladies Who Supported the Southern Confederacy

*Five-Star Books & Gifts From the Heart of the American South*

**SeaRavenPress.com**

# THE BATTLE OF
# SPRING HILL

*Recollections of Confederate & Union Soldiers*

COLLECTED, ARRANGED, & EDITED, WITH AN INTRODUCTION & SUMMARY
BY THE AUTHOR, "THE VOICE OF THE TRADITIONAL SOUTH," COLONEL

# LOCHLAINN SEABROOK

JEFFERSON DAVIS HISTORICAL GOLD MEDAL WINNER

Generously Illustrated and Diligently
Researched for the Elucidation of the Reader

2018

Sea Raven Press, Nashville, Tennessee, USA

# THE BATTLE OF SPRING HILL

Published by
Sea Raven Press, Cassidy Ravensdale, President
PO Box 1484, Spring Hill, Tennessee 37174-1484 USA
SeaRavenPress.com • searavenpress@gmail.com

Copyright © 2018 Lochlainn Seabrook
in accordance with U.S. and international copyright laws and regulations, as stated and protected under the Berne Union for the Protection of Literary and Artistic Property (Berne Convention), and the Universal Copyright Convention (the UCC). All rights reserved under the Pan-American and International Copyright Conventions.

1st SRP paperback edition, 1st printing, July 2018 • ISBN: 978-1-943737-69-7
1st SRP hardcover edition, 1st printing, July 2018 • ISBN: 978-1-943737-70-3

ISBN: 978-1-943737-69-7 (paperback)
Library of Congress Control Number: 2018949382

This work is the copyrighted intellectual property of Lochlainn Seabrook and has been registered with the Copyright Office at the Library of Congress in Washington, D.C., USA. No part of this work (including text, covers, drawings, photos, illustrations, maps, images, diagrams, etc.), in whole or in part, may be used, reproduced, stored in a retrieval system, or transmitted, in any form or by any means now known or hereafter invented, without written permission from the publisher. The sale, duplication, hire, lending, copying, digitalization, or reproduction of this material, in any manner or form whatsoever, is also prohibited, and is a violation of federal, civil, and digital copyright law, which provides severe civil and criminal penalties for any violations.

The Battle of Spring Hill: Recollections of Confederate and Union Soldiers, by Lochlainn Seabrook. Includes endnotes, maps, and bibliographical references.

*Front and back cover design and art, book design, layout, and interior art by Lochlainn Seabrook*
*All images, graphic design, graphic art, and illustrations copyright © Lochlainn Seabrook*
*All images selected, placed, manipulated, and/or created by Lochlainn Seabrook*
*Cover images and design copyright © Lochlainn Seabrook*

All persons who approve of the authority and principles of Colonel Lochlainn Seabrook's literary work, and realize its benefits as a means of reeducating the world about the South and the Confederacy, are hereby requested to avidly recommend his books to others and to vigorously cooperate in extending their reach, scope, and influence around the globe.

The views on the American "Civil War" documented in this book are those of the publisher.

PRINTED & MANUFACTURED IN OCCUPIED TENNESSEE, FORMER CONFEDERATE STATES OF AMERICA

# Dedication

To my Confederate relatives, as well as the thousands of other patriotic Southern soldiers, who were present at the Battle of Spring Hill, Tennessee, in the Fall of 1864. Your heroism, your memory, and your service in the cause of preserving America's constitutional principles will never be forgotten.

# Epigraph

The inaction just at the most critical moment of the Army of Tennessee has never been explained, and may never be. It seemed fate.

*Sumner A. Cunningham*
CONFEDERATE SOLDIER, 1910

# CONTENTS

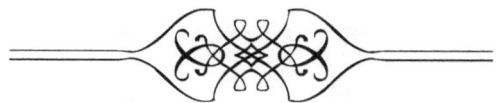

*Notes to the Reader* - 11
*Introduction, by Lochlainn Seabrook* - 15
*Some Officers of Note at Spring Hill* - 17
*Maps* - 18

SECTION 1: CONFEDERATE RECOLLECTIONS - 23
SECTION 2: UNION RECOLLECTIONS - 109
SUMMARY: BY LOCHLAINN SEABROOK - 129

*Notes* - 133
*Bibliography* - 135
*Meet the Author* - 139

## Keep Your Body, Mind, & Spirit Vibrating at Their Highest Level

YOU CAN DO SO BY READING THE BOOKS OF

# SEA RAVEN PRESS

There is nothing that will so perfectly keep your body, mind, and spirit in a healthy condition as to think wisely and positively. Hence you should not only read this book, but also the other books that we offer. They will quicken your physical, mental, and spiritual vibrations, enabling you to maintain a position in society as a healthy erudite person.

## KEEP YOURSELF WELL-INFORMED!

The well-informed person is always at the head of the procession, while the ignorant, the lazy, and the unthoughtful hang onto the rear. If you are a Spiritual man or woman, do yourself a great favor: read Sea Raven Press books and stay well posted on the Truth. It is almost criminal for one to remain in ignorance while the opportunity to gain knowledge is open to all at a nominal price.

We invite you to visit our Webstore for a wide selection of wholesome, family-friendly, well-researched, educational books for all ages. You will be glad you did!

*Five-Star Books & Gifts From the Heart of the American South*

# SeaRavenPress.com

# NOTES TO THE READER

"NOTHING IN THE PAST IS DEAD TO THE MAN WHO WOULD
LEARN HOW THE PRESENT CAME TO BE WHAT IT IS."

WILLIAM STUBBS, VICTORIAN ENGLISH HISTORIAN

THE TWO MAIN POLITICAL PARTIES IN 1860

☞ In any study of America's antebellum, bellum, and postbellum periods, it is vitally important to understand that in 1860 the two major political parties—the Democrats and the newly formed Republicans—were the opposite of what they are today. In other words, the Democrats of the mid 19th Century were Conservatives, akin to the Republican Party of today, while the Republicans of the mid 19th Century were Liberals, akin to the Democratic Party of today.[1]

The author's cousin, Confederate Vice President and Democrat Alexander H. Stephens: a Southern Conservative.

Thus the Confederacy's Democratic president, Jefferson Davis, was a Conservative (with libertarian leanings); the Union's Republican president, Abraham Lincoln, was a Liberal (with socialistic leanings).[2] This is why, in the mid 1800s, the conservative wing of the Democratic Party was known as "the States' Rights Party."[3]

Hence, the Democrats of the Civil War period referred to themselves as "conservatives," "confederates," "anti-centralists," or "constitutionalists" (the latter because they favored strict adherence to the original Constitution—which tacitly guaranteed states' rights—as created by the Founding Fathers), while the Republicans called themselves "liberals," "nationalists," "centralists," or "consolidationists" (the latter three because they wanted to nationalize the central government and consolidate political power in Washington, D.C.).[4]

Since this idea is new to most of my readers, let us further demystify it by viewing it from the perspective of the American Revolutionary War. If Davis and his conservative Southern constituents (the Democrats of 1861) had been alive in 1775, they would have sided with George Washington and the American colonists, who sought to secede from the tyrannical government of Great Britain; if Lincoln and his Liberal Northern constituents (the Republicans of 1861) had been alive at that time, they would have sided with King George III and the English monarchy, who sought to maintain the American colonies as possessions of the British Empire. It is due to this very comparison that Southerners often refer to their secession as the Second Declaration of Independence and the "Civil War" as the Second American Revolutionary War.

Without a basic understanding of these facts, the American "Civil War" will forever remain incomprehensible. For a full discussion of this topic see my book, *Abraham Lincoln Was a Liberal, Jefferson Davis Was a Conservative: The Missing Key to Understanding the American Civil War.*

## A WORD ON EARLY AMERICAN MATERIAL

☛ In order to preserve the authentic historicity of the antebellum, bellum, and postbellum periods, I have retained the original spellings, formatting, and punctuation of the early Americans I quote. These include such items as British-English spellings, long-running paragraphs, obsolete words, and various literary devices peculiar to the time. However, I have corrected misspelled names to prevent confusion, and also *where possible*, inaccurate dates and locations (the inevitable result of old faulty memories). Bracketed words within quotes are my additions and clarifications, while italicized words within quotes are (where indicated) my emphasis.

## PRESENTISM

☛ As a historian I view *presentism* (judging the past according to present day mores and customs) as the enemy of authentic history. And this is precisely why enemies of the South employ it in its ongoing war against traditional American, conservative, and Christian

Judging our ancestors by our own standards is unfair, unjust, misleading, and unethical.

values. By looking at history through the lens of modern day beliefs—and, just as heinous, fabricating obviously fake history based on emotion, opinion, and political ideology—they are able to distort, revise, and reshape the past into a false narrative that fits their ideological agenda: the liberalization *and* Northernization of America, the enlargement and further centralization of the national government, and total control of American political, economic, and social power, the same agenda that Liberal Lincoln championed.[5]

This book rejects presentism and replaces it with what I call *historicalism*: judging our ancestors based on the values of their own time. To get the most from this work the reader is invited to reject presentism as well. In this way—along with casting aside preconceived notions and the bogus "history" churned out by our left-wing education system—the truth in this work will be most readily ascertained and absorbed; truth that has been rigorously researched and forensically uncovered by myself using the scientific method. As Confederate Colonel Bennett H. Young noted in 1901:

> History is valuable only as it is true. Opinions concerning acts are not history; acts themselves alone are historic.[6]

## LEARN MORE

☛ The American "Civil War," in reality, the War Over the Constitution, can never be fully understood without a thorough knowledge of the South's perspective. As this book is only meant to be a brief introductory guide to these topics, one cannot hope to learn the complete story here. For those who are interested in additional material from Dixie's viewpoint, please see my comprehensive histories listed on pages 2 and 3.

# 14 ∾ THE BATTLE OF SPRING HILL

Why the South fought . . .

# INTRODUCTION

**W**HY IS A STUDY OF the Battle of Spring Hill important? Why does this seemingly minuscule military engagement still matter in the 21st Century? Indeed, a tourist driving through Spring Hill on Highway 31 today would be forgiven for not even knowing that a Civil War battle took place here. Many of the city's newer residents are certainly not aware of it—and for good reason: as of this

(Photo Lochlainn Seabrook)

writing there is not a single sign on Main Street clearly acknowledging it, while the few signs that do are located mainly on the town's back roads.

And this is the second tragedy of the Battle of Spring Hill: the downplaying of its significance. Mainstream historians still cavalierly refer to it as "one of the most controversial *non-fighting* events of the entire war,"[7] this despite the reality that much fighting *did* take place, with hundreds of soldiers on both sides injured, killed, or missing. The very reason for the battle is usually not even understood, and so it is simply ignored. Obviously it was not about slavery or "preserving the Union."[8] In actuality the Battle of Spring Hill was a small but important aspect of the much larger war the South was waging, one commonly known as the "Southern Cause." And what was that cause?

It was Americanism, which is another word for Conservatism! (Note: The Democrats and Republicans were reversed in the 1860s.)[9] As nearly every Victorian Southerner attested before, during, and after the War, the Confederate States took up arms in an effort to preserve both the *original Constitution* (which Lincoln and other Northern Liberals had promised to overturn)[10] and the delicate *balance of power* between the Conservative South and the Liberal North as it had been established by America's Founding Fathers.[11] Let us examine these well established facts in the context of the Battle of Spring Hill.

The Confederates' "lost opportunity" at Spring Hill on November 29, 1864, set the stage for the tragic and massive Confederate loss the following day at Franklin, where five Southern generals were killed and a sixth expired shortly thereafter of his injuries—one of the largest, if not the largest, number of officerial casualties in any known battle. In all, some 1,750 Confederates perished on the fields of Franklin on November 30th, and at a rate of 350 per hour, making it the Civil War's bloodiest battle, as more died here in a shorter amount of time than in any other contest.[12]

(Photo Lochlainn Seabrook)

Just as significant, while Spring Hill led to the Franklin debacle (in which Confederate General John Bell Hood needlessly marched his soldiers over an open, two-mile wide plain surrounded by well entrenched Yankees), Franklin in turn led to the disaster at Nashville a few weeks later (December 15-16, 1864), where the Confederacy suffered an estimated additional 4,500 casualties, and Hood and the tattered remains of the Army of Tennessee were chased south all the way to Alabama. Demoralized and humiliated, on January 13, 1865, Hood asked to be relieved of his command, and the Army of Tennessee was turned over to the son of U.S. President Zachary Taylor, Confederate General Richard Taylor. The South would not recover.[13]

Oaklawn, Hood's headquarters during the Battle of Spring Hill. (Photo Lochlainn Seabrook)

The calamitous outcome of Hood's Tennessee Campaign (for us, beginning with the "lost opportunity" at Spring Hill) has been rightly called "the turning point of the War in the West." For Hood himself it "seems to have been the sore point of his whole military career."[14] It was certainly no accident that the Civil War itself came to an end only four months later at Appomattox.

Just what was the "lost opportunity"? Why is it called "the great mystery of the War"? How and why did it occur? Who was ultimately responsible?

As there was no clear cut answer in 1864, and as there is still no agreement among military historians on these questions today, we can hardly hope to answer them in this small book.[15] Nonetheless, I believe that the Confederate and Union veterans whose words I have selected to fill it will shed light on the vital subject of the Battle of Spring Hill, an encounter whose military movements one writer in this volume correctly notes

> have been more persistently and heatedly discussed, not only by the leaders of the contending armies but within those armies themselves, up to this very day, than any operations of any army during the Civil War.

It is my hope that this work will revive interest in both this seldom discussed but influential conflict and the men who fought in it. An honorable people honors its military dead with monuments, speeches, and wreaths, whatever the color of their uniforms or the nature of their political views.

Lochlainn Seabrook
Nashville, Tennessee, USA
July 2018
*In Nobis Regnat Christus*

# SOME OFFICERS OF NOTE AT SPRING HILL

NOTES: PARTIAL LIST. ALPHABETIZED. SOME MEN MAY NOT HAVE ACTUALLY BEEN PRESENT, BUT THEIR REGIMENTS WERE.

Gen. John Bell Hood, Confederate Commander at Spring Hill, Army of Tennessee, C.S.A.

Maj. Gen. John M. Schofield, Union Commander, 4th and 23rd Army Corps, U.S.A.

## CONFEDERACY

Armstrong, Gen. Frank C.
Bate, Gen. William B.
Bell, Gen. Tyree H.
Biffle, Col. Jacob B.
Bostick, Maj. Joseph
Brown, Gen. John C.
Buford, Gen. Abraham
Bullock, Gen. Robert
Capers, Gen. Ellison
Carter, Gen. John C.
Cheatham, Gen. Benjamin F.
Cleburne, Gen. Patrick R.
Crossland, Col. Edward
Forrest, Gen. Nathan B.
Gist, Gen. States Rights
Gordon, Gen. George W.
Govan, Gen. Daniel C.
Granbury, Gen. Hiram B.
Hood, Gen. John Bell
Jackson, Gen. William H.
Johnson, Gen. Edward
Lee, Gen. Stephen D.
Lowrey, Gen. Mark P.
Manigault, Gen. Arthur M.
Pettus, Gen. Edmund W.
Ross, Gen. Lawrence S.
Rucker, Col. Edmund W.
Sharp, Gen. Jacob H.
Smith, Gen. James A.
Stewart, Gen. Alexander P.
Strahl, Gen. Otho F.
Vaulx, Maj. Joseph

## UNION

Atwater, Maj. Frederick A.
Bradley, Gen. Luther P.
Bridges, Capt. Lyman
Brown, Lieut. Col. Robert C.
Buckner, Col. Allen
Canby, Lieut. Samuel
Capron, Col. Horace
Caswell, Lieut. Thomas D.
Conrad, Col. Joseph
Coon, Gen. Datus E.
Cox, Gen. Jacob D.
Croxton, Gen. John T.
Garrard, Gen. Kenner
Hatch, Gen. Edward
Kimball, Gen. Nathan
Lane, Col. John Q.
Marshall, Capt. Alexander
Moore, Gen. Jonathan B.
Opdycke, Gen. Emerson
Ruger, Gen. Thomas H.
Schofield, Gen. John M.
Scoville, Lieut. Charles W.
Smith, Maj. Orlow
Stanley, Gen. David S.
Strickland, Col. S. A.
Twining, Capt. William J.
Wagner, Gen. George D.
Whitaker, Gen. Walter C.
Wilson, Gen. James H.
Wood, Gen. Thomas J.
Young, Maj. J. Morris
Ziegler, Capt. Jacob

# MAPS

Middle Tennessee and Northern Alabama. Spring Hill is just below Nashville and Franklin on the Columbia Pike (modern Highway 31).

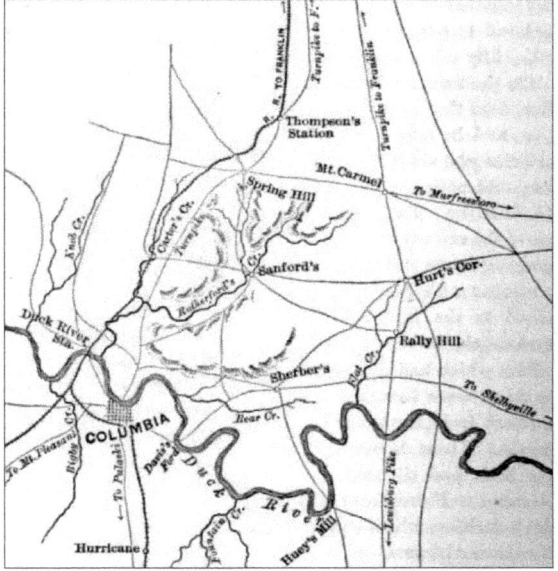

Vicinity of Columbia, Tennessee, 1860s.

Columbia to Spring Hill on the Columbia Pike.

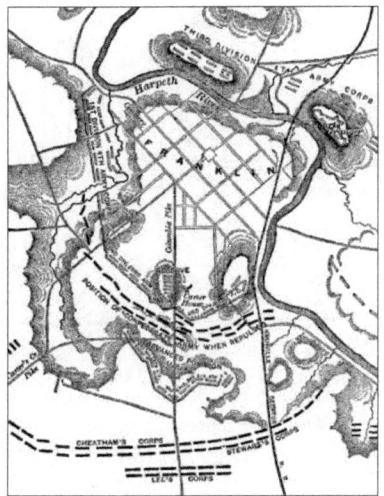
Map of the Battle of Franklin, November 30, 1864. The Confederate failure at Spring Hill led to the Confederate tragedy at Franklin, and Franklin led to the Confederate disaster at Nashville, December 15-16.

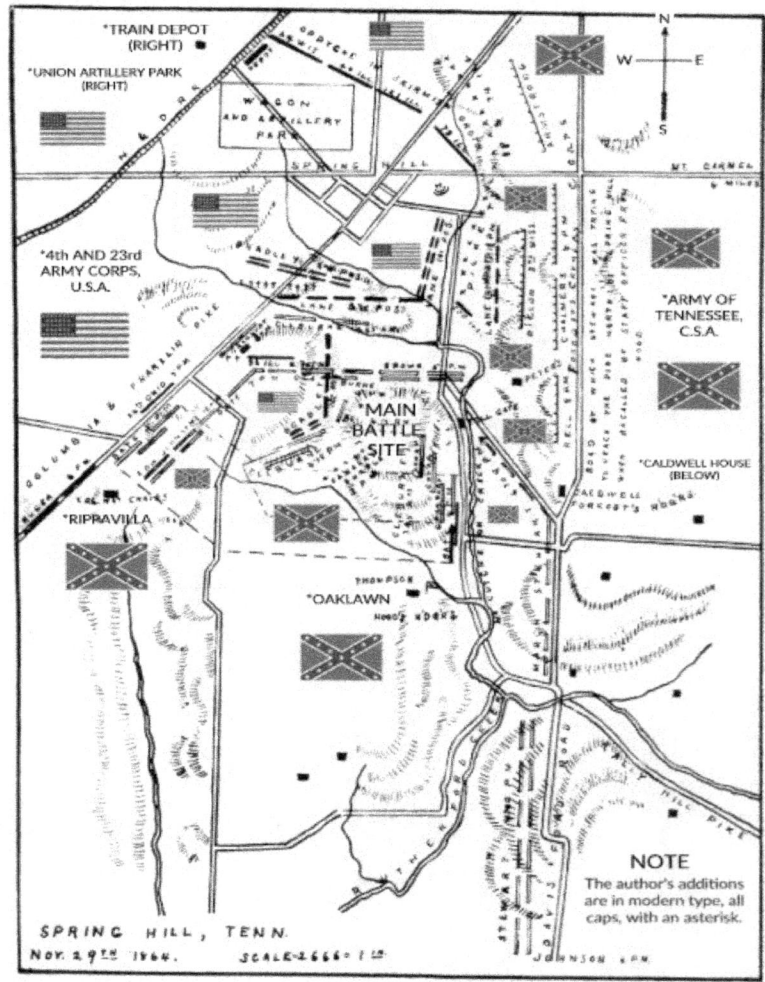

Map of the Battle of Spring Hill, November 29, 1864 (created circa 1908), showing Confederate and Union positions in and around the town as they appeared that day. I have added information, including Confederate and Union Flags, to aid the reader in understanding the layout. Although there was some overlap, generally speaking the Confederates formed on and operated primarily out of the east and south; the Yankees formed on and operated primarily out of the west and north. Spring Hill looks substantially different today, with many new inhabitants, streets, stores, churches, and sections, all which have expanded outward from the center. While many of the roads shown on the map still exist, some have been renamed.

# SECTION 1
# CONFEDERATE RECOLLECTIONS

Historical marker at the Battle of Spring Hill site, Spring Hill, TN. (Photo Lochlainn Seabrook)

# CONFEDERATE RECOLLECTIONS

John Bell Hood

## J. B. HOOD'S DESCRIPTION OF THE BATTLE OF SPRING HILL

☛ . . . On the 20th of November, Stewart's Corps having crossed the Tennessee and bivouacked several miles beyond on the Lawrenceburg road, orders were issued that the entire Army move at an early hour the next morning. Lee's and Stewart's Corps marched upon the Chisholm and the Lawrenceburg roads, and Cheatham's Corps upon the Waynesboro road.

Early dawn of the 21st found the Army in motion. I hoped by a rapid march to get in rear of Schofield's forces, then at Pulaski, before they were able to reach Duck river. That night headquarters were established at Rawhide, twelve miles north of Florence, on the Waynesboro road.

The march was resumed on the 22nd, and continued till the 27th, upon which date the troops, having taken advantage of every available road, reached Columbia, via Mount Pleasant. Forrest operated in our front against the enemy's cavalry which he easily drove from one position to another.

The Federals at Pulaski became alarmed, and, by forced marches day and night, reached Columbia, upon Duck river, just in time to prevent our troops from cutting them off. Van Horne, in his *History of the Army of the Cumberland*, thus mentions their narrow escape:

> General Hood's rapid advance had been made with the hope of cutting off

General Schofield from Columbia, and barely failed in this object, as the National troops gained the place by a night march.

The enemy having formed line of battle around Columbia, Lee's Corps filed into position with its right upon the Mount Pleasant pike; Stewart's formed on Lee's right, his own right flank extending to the Pulaski pike; and Cheatham established his left on the latter pike, with his right resting on Duck river. Army headquarters were established at the residence of Mrs. Warfield, about three miles south of Columbia.

The two Armies lay opposite each other during the 27$^{th}$. The Federals being entrenched, I determined not to attack them in their breastworks, if I could possibly avoid it, but to permit them to cross undisturbed to the north bank of Duck river that night, as I supposed they would do; to hasten preparations, and endeavor to place the main body of the Confederate Army at Spring Hill, twelve miles directly in the enemy's rear, and about mid-way upon the only pike leading to Franklin; to attack as the Federals retreated, and put to rout and capture, if possible, their Army which was the sole obstacle between our forces and Nashville—in truth, the only barrier to the success of the campaign.

I was confident that after Schofield had crossed the river and placed that obstruction between our respective Armies, he would feel in security, and would remain in his position at least a sufficient length of time to allow me to throw pontoons across the river about three miles above his left flank, and, by a bold and rapid march together with heavy demonstrations in his front, gain his rear before he was fully apprised of my object.

The situation presented an occasion for one of those interesting and beautiful moves upon the chess-board of war, to perform which I had often desired an opportunity. As stated in a letter to General Longstreet, I urgently appealed for authority to turn the Federal left at Round Top Mountain. I had beheld with admiration the noble deeds and grand results achieved by the immortal Jackson in similar manœuvres; I had seen his Corps made equal to ten times its number by a sudden attack on the enemy's rear, and I hoped in this instance to be able to profit by the teaching of my illustrious countryman. As I apprehended unnecessary and fatal delay might be occasioned by the appearance of the enemy on the line of march to the rear, I decided to bridge the river that night, and move at dawn the next morning with Cheatham's Corps—whose right was then resting near the point selected for a crossing—together with Stewart's Corps and Johnston's Division, of Lee's Corps, and to leave Lieutenant General Lee with Stevenson's and Clayton's Divisions and the bulk of the artillery, to demonstrate heavily against Schofield, and follow him if he retired.

Since I had attempted this same movement on the 22$^{nd}$ of July, and had been unable to secure its success, I resolved to go in person at the head of the advance brigade, and lead the Army to Spring Hill.

Colonel Prestman and his assistants laid the pontoons during the night of the 28th, about three miles above Columbia; orders to move at dawn the following day having been issued to the two corps and the division above mentioned, I rode with my staff to Cheatham's right, passed over the bridge soon after daybreak, and moved forward at the head of Granberry's Texas brigade, of Cleburne's Division, with instructions that the remaining corps and divisions follow, and at the same time keep well closed up during the march.

General Forrest had crossed the evening previous and moved to the front and right. I threw forward a few skirmishers who advanced at as rapid a pace as I supposed the troops could possibly proceed.

The Duck River as it looks today, Columbia, TN. (Photo Lochlainn Seabrook)

During the march, the Federal cavalry appeared on the hills to our left; not a moment, however, was lost on that account, as the Army was marching by the right flank and was prepared to face at any instant in their direction. No attention, therefore, was paid to the enemy, save to throw out a few sharp-shooters in his front. I well knew that to stop and lose time in reconnoitering would defeat my object, which was to reach the enemy's rear and cut him off from Nashville.

I also knew that Schofield was occupied in his front, since I could distinctly hear the roar of Lee's artillery at Columbia, whilst a feint was made to cross the river.

Thus I led the main body of the Army to within about two miles and in full view of the pike from Columbia to Spring Hill and Franklin. I here halted about 3 p.m., and requested General Cheatham, commanding the leading corps, and Major General Cleburne to advance to the spot where, sitting upon my horse, I had in sight the enemy's wagons and men passing at double-quick along the Franklin pike. As these officers approached, I spoke to Cheatham in the following words which I quote almost verbatim, as they have remained indelibly engraved upon my memory ever since that fatal day: "General, do you see the enemy there, retreating rapidly to escape us?" He answered in the affirmative. "Go," I continued, " with your Corps, take possession of and hold that pike at or near Spring Hill. Accept whatever comes, and turn all those wagons over to our side of the house."

Then addressing Cleburne, I said, "General, you have heard the orders just given. You have one of my best divisions. Go with General Cheatham, assist him in every way you can, and do as he directs." Again, as a parting injunction to them, I added, "Go and do this at once. Stewart is near at hand, and I will have him double-quick his men to the front."

They immediately sent staff officers to hurry the men forward, and moved off with their troops at a quick pace in the direction of the enemy. I dispatched several of my staff to the rear, with orders to Stewart and Johnson to make all possible haste. Meantime I rode to one side, and looked on at Cleburne's Division, followed by the remainder of Cheatham's Corps, as it marched by seemingly ready for battle.

Within about one-half hour from the time Cheatham left me, skirmishing began with the enemy, when I rode forward to a point nearer the pike, and again sent a staff officer to Stewart and Johnson to push forward. At the same time, I dispatched a messenger to General Cheatham to lose no time in gaining possession of the pike at Spring Hill. It was reported back that he was about to do so.

Listening attentively to the fire of the skirmishers in that direction, I discovered there was no continued roar of musketry, and being aware of the quick approach of darkness, after four o'clock at that season of the year, I became somewhat uneasy, and again ordered an officer to go to General Cheatham, inform him that his supports were very near at hand, that he must attack at once, if he had not already so done, and take and hold possession of the pike. Shortly afterwards, I entrusted another officer with the same message, and, if my memory is not treacherous, finally requested the Governor of Tennessee, Isham G. Harris, to hasten forward and impress upon Cheatham the importance of action without delay. I knew no large force of the enemy could be at Spring Hill, as couriers reported Schofield's main body still in front of Lee, at Columbia, up to a late hour in the day. I thought it probable that Cheatham had taken possession of Spring Hill without encountering material opposition, or had formed line across the pike, north of the town, and entrenched without coming in serious contact with the enemy, which would account for the little musketry heard in his direction. However, to ascertain the truth, I sent an officer to ask Cheatham if he held the pike, and to inform him of the arrival of Stewart, whose Corps I intended to throw on his left, in order to assail the Federals in flank that evening or the next morning, as they approached and formed to attack Cheatham. At this juncture, the last messenger returned with the report that the road had not been taken possession of. General Stewart was then ordered to proceed to the right of Cheatham and place his Corps across the pike, north of Spring Hill.

By this hour, however, twilight was upon us, when General Cheatham rode up in person. I at once directed Stewart to halt, and, turning to

Cheatham, I exclaimed with deep emotion, as I felt the golden opportunity fast slipping from me, "General, why in the name of God have you not attacked the enemy, and taken possession of that pike ?" He replied that the line looked a little too long for him, and that Stewart should first form on his right. I could hardly believe it possible that this brave old soldier, who had given proof of such courage and ability upon so many hard-fought fields, would even make such a report. After leading him within full view of the enemy, and pointing out to him the Federals, retreating in great haste and confusion, along the pike, and then giving explicit orders to attack, I would as soon have expected midday to turn into darkness as for him to have disobeyed my orders. I then asked General Cheatham whether or not Stewart's Corps, if formed on the right, would extend across the pike. He answered in the affirmative. Guides were at once furnished to point out Cheatham's right to General Stewart, who was ordered to form thereon, with his right extending across the pike. Darkness, however, which was increased by large shade trees in that vicinity, soon closed upon us, and Stewart's Corps, after much annoyance, went into bivouac for the night, near but not across the pike, at about eleven or twelve o'clock.

(Photo Lochlainn Seabrook)

It was reported to me after this hour that the enemy was marching along the road, almost under the light of the campfires of the main body of the Army. I sent anew to General Cheatham to know if at least a line of skirmishers could not be advanced, in order to throw the Federals in confusion, to delay their march, and allow us a chance to attack in the morning. Nothing was done. The Federals, with immense wagon trains, were permitted to march by us the remainder of the night, within gunshot of our lines. I could not succeed in arousing the troops to action, when one good division would have sufficed to do the work. One good division, I re-assert, could have routed that portion of the enemy which was at Spring Hill; have taken possession of and formed line across the road; and thus have made it an easy matter to Stewart's Corps, Johnston's Division, and Lee's two Divisions from Columbia, to have enveloped, routed, and captured Schofield's Army that afternoon and the ensuing day. General Forrest gallantly opposed the enemy further down to our right to the full extent of his power; beyond this effort, nothing whatever was done, although never was a grander opportunity offered to utterly rout and destroy the Federal Army.

Had I dreamed one moment that Cheatham would have failed to give battle, or at least to take position across the pike and force the enemy to assault him, I would have ridden, myself, to the front, and led the troops into action. Although it is right and proper that a Commander-in-Chief, in the event of disaster to a portion of his line during an engagement, should endeavor in person to rally the troops, it is not expected nor considered expedient that he should inaugurate a battle by leading a division or brigade. Had I done so, my opponents would have just cause for the charge of recklessness. I would, nevertheless, have risked my life in this instance, had I conceived the possibility of the disregard of my orders, on the part of this officer. General Lee was in a measure thwarted by the same want of prompt action, at Gettysburg. Whilst I failed utterly to bring on battle at Spring Hill, he was unable to get the corps of his Army to attack and co-operate, as desired. He was thus checkmated for two days, and finally lost the battle. Had our immortal Chieftain foreseen the result of this inactivity, he would, doubtless, have ordered and acted differently.

Before proceeding further, I will produce additional evidence from Federal sources, in order to make still more manifest the opportunity which was lost to the Confederate arms on the 29th of November, at Spring Hill.

Shortly after the war, I met in New Orleans Colonel Fullerton, of the United States Army; he was Schofield's adjutant general at the time of these events, in connection with which he wrote me the following:

> New Orleans, La., October 20th, 1865. To General Hood. General: The only body of United States troops on the battlefield of Spring Hill, Tennessee, on the 29th of November, 1864, was the Second Division of the Fourth Army Corps. I think the division was less than four thousand (4000) strong. There were no other United States troops in or about Spring Hill on that day but one or two hundred cavalrymen and perhaps fifty or sixty infantrymen (post troops). The rest of General Schofield's Army was in the vicinity of Columbia, on the north side of Duck river, and none of these troops began to arrive at Spring Hill until after 9 p.m. I arrived in Spring Hill with the Second Division of the Fourth Corps, and remained there till nearly daylight when I went to Franklin with the rear of the Army. I was at the time lieutenant colonel and assistant adjutant general of the Fourth Army Corps. J. S. Fullerton, Brevet Brigadier General, United States Volunteers.

Van Horne, in his *History of the Army of the Cumberland* [U.S.], informs us that at 3 p.m., when the Confederate Army was already at Spring Hill, the Federal commander became apprised of our move in his rear, and thus describes his retreat:

His (Lee's) repeated attacks were all repulsed by General Cox, and at 3 p.m., General Schofield became satisfied that the enemy would not attack on Duck river, but was moving two corps directly on Spring Hill. He then gave orders for the withdrawal.

. . . There was some delay at Rutherford's creek, as the bridge was inadequate for the emergency, but nevertheless the divisions, one after another, arrived at Spring Hill—the foremost of the three at 11 p.m. The enemy's pickets fired into the column frequently, but as they did not come upon the road, the National troops gave no response. The enemy were so close to the road, that when a column was not moving upon it, it was difficult for a single horseman to pass. . . . There was momentary expectation that this great Army would take a step forward, and press troops, artillery, and trains from the road in confusion and rout; but still the movement went on without interruption by the enemy.

Rarely has an Army escaped so easily from a peril so threatening.

In connection with this grave misfortune, I must here record an act of candor and nobility upon the part of General Cheatham, which proves him to be equally generous-hearted and brave. I was, necessarily, much pained by the disappointment suffered, and, a few days later, telegraphed to Richmond, to withdraw my previous recommendation for his promotion, and to request that another be assigned to the command of his Corps. Before the receipt of a reply, this officer called at my headquarters—then at the residence of Mr. Overton [Travellers' Rest], six miles from Nashville—and, standing in my presence, spoke an honest avowal of his error, in the acknowledgment that he felt we had lost a brilliant opportunity at Spring Hill to deal the enemy a crushing blow, and that he was greatly to blame. I telegraphed and wrote to the War Department to withdraw my application for his removal, in the belief that, inspired with an ambition to retrieve his short-coming, he would prove in the future doubly zealous in the service of his country. The following are the dispatches above referred to:

Travellers' Rest, Nashville, TN. (Photo Lochlainn Seabrook)

> Headquarters, Six Miles from Nashville, On Franklin Pike, December 7th, 1864. Honorable J. A. Seddon: I withdraw my recommendation, in favor of the promotion of Major General Cheatham for reasons which I will write more fully. J. B. Hood, General.

> Headquarters, Six Miles from Nashville, On Franklin Pike, December 8th, 1864. Honorable J. A. Seddon, Secretary of War [C.S.A.]; General G. T. Beauregard, Macon, Ga.: A good Lieutenant General should be sent here at

once to command the corps now commanded by Major General Cheatham. I have no one to recommend for the position. J. B. Hood, General.

Headquarters, Six Miles from Nashville, On Franklin Pike, December 8th, 1864. Honorable J. A. Seddon: Major General Cheatham made a failure on the 30th of November, which will be a lesson to him. I think it best he should remain in his position for the present. I withdraw my telegrams of yesterday and to-day on this subject. J. B. Hood, General.

On the 11th of December I wrote the Hon. Mr. Seddon:

Major General Cheatham has frankly confessed the great error of which he was guilty, and attaches much blame to himself. While his error lost so much to the country, it has been a severe lesson to him, by which he will profit in the future. In consideration of this, and of his previous conduct, I think that it is best that he should retain, for the present, the command he now holds.

The best move in my career as a soldier, I was thus destined to behold come to naught. The discovery that the Army, after a forward march of one hundred and eighty miles, was still, seemingly, unwilling to accept battle unless under the protection of breastworks, caused me to experience grave concern. In my inmost heart I questioned whether or not I would ever succeed in eradicating this evil. It seemed to me I had exhausted every means in the power of one man to remove this stumbling block to the Army of Tennessee. And I will here inquire, in vindication of its fair name, if any intelligent man of that Army supposes one moment that these same troops, one year previous, would, even without orders to attack, have allowed the enemy to pass them at Rocky-faced Ridge, as he did at Spring Hill.

Stephen Dill Lee.

Lieutenant General Lee performed his duty, at Columbia, with great skill and fidelity which were crowned with entire success: he attained the object of the demonstration, which was to keep the Federals in ignorance of our movements till sufficient time had been allowed the Army to reach the desired point. Colonel Beckham, chief of artillery in Lee's Corps, and one of the most promising officers of his rank, was unfortunately killed on the 29th, during the heavy cannonade in front of that town. On the morning of the 30th of November, Lee was on the march up the Franklin pike, when the main body of the Army, at Spring Hill, awoke to find the Federals had disappeared.

I hereupon decided, before the enemy would be able to reach his stronghold at Nashville, to make that same afternoon another and final effort to overtake and rout him, and drive him in the Big Harpeth river at Franklin, since I could no longer hope to get between him and Nashville, by reason of the short distance from Franklin to that city, and the advantage which the Federals enjoyed in the possession of the direct road.[16] — JOHN BELL HOOD, CONFEDERATE COMMANDER

## HOOD'S FAILURE AT SPRING HILL

☞ On November 27, at night, the Federal army, after a day of heavy skirmishing with Hood's Infantry, abandoned Columbia and took a strong position on the north side of Duck River, several hundred yards from the stream, while the cavalry under Wilson, who assumed command on November 24 greatly reenforced, spread out eastward for some ten miles, guarding the fords on Duck River and watching that flank of the army. On that night, November 27, General Hood conceived the idea of a flank movement to the rightward of Columbia and a rapid march upon the enemy's line of communication at or about Spring Hill, some sixteen miles to the northward. This would seem to be a most difficult undertaking, when it is remembered that Gen. James H. Wilson, a brave and capable cavalry officer, guarded that flank with more than seven thousand cavalry, which was being constantly reenforced, and was led by Hatch, Harrison, Coon, Croxton, Capron, Johnson, and Garrard, all trained and experienced cavalry leaders. The movement was, as we shall presently see, fraught with momentous consequences to both armies, and resulted in certain movements on the chessboard of war that have been more persistently and heatedly discussed, not only by the leaders of the contending armies but within those armies themselves, up to this very day, than any operations of any army during the Civil War.

A most brilliant movement was made by a great army [Confederate] on its enemy's [Union] flank and rear. The enemy's artillery, ordnance, and supply trains were reached, guarded by one division only of 5,689 men, the attacking force numbering two army corps and one division of infantry and a corps of cavalry, aggregating more than 25,000 men. And then a sort of paralysis fell upon the whole assailing force, which deliberately encamped, and not only allowed the train guard of one division to march off, but the enemy's entire army to come up from below and pass quietly by in the nighttime without a gun being fired at them except by some skirmishers and one restless brigade of Forrest's Cavalry, which came near demoralizing the whole retreating army, already terrified at its perilous position. Somebody had blundered in each army.

Volumes have been written in heated controversy over this strange occurrence by men of both armies, and yet no one has disclosed the true reason for the mishap to the Confederate army at what a Federal writer calls "this interesting and instructive conjuncture," and which was, in fact, the turning point of the war in the West. Hood, successful here, would have taken his place as one of the great captains of the war. Schofield, successful in eluding his able but unfortunate antagonist through the sheerest good fortune, became subsequently commander in chief of the armies of the United States.

It is the purpose of the writer to follow circumstantially in detail all the movements of this remarkable operation, quoting liberally from the contemporaneous letters and dispatches of the several actors, in order to throw light on the motives for the various maneuvers combinations, and actions recorded, and to trace hour by hour on corrected maps the several positions of the different corps and divisions of both armies as the best means of illustrating the curious story of the fateful undertaking and its results. This faithfully done, it is believed that here will be little left to controversy in the future.

The morning of November 28 found the two armies stationed, as above indicated, on opposite sides of Duck River and in and around Columbia. Forrest's Cavalry, under that skillful leader, had been concentrated the night before, after being relieved from the skirmish line by Hood's Infantry, on Fountain Creek, some five miles southeast of Columbia. The three divisions of Chalmers, Buford, and Jackson, with Biffles's small command, numbered about 5,500 troopers fairly well mounted and equipped.

(Photo Lochlainn Seabrook)

On the morning of the 28th Forrest was early afield, his three divisions moving rapidly in an easterly direction south of Duck River toward the several fords selected for the crossings. There were no bridges and the river was much swollen with the recent rains, so much so indeed that General Wilson accepted the opinion of citizens that the crossings were unfordable. But Forrest, to whom even large rivers seemed to offer little impediment, pushed rapidly on, and before 4 p.m. had crossed two of the divisions, Chalmers fording the stream at Carr's Mill, seven miles east of Columbia, and Jackson at Lillard's Mill, east of the Lewisburg and Franklin Pikes. Buford, who attempted to cross at Hardison's Mill, the crossing of the Lewisburg and Franklin Turnpike, was confronted by Capron's Brigade, now reenforced to some 1,800 men by the arrival of the 5$^{th}$ Iowa and 7$^{th}$ Ohio Regiments, and was unable up to nightfall to force a passage. But Jackson, who had crossed at Lillard's Mill, an old mill site four miles above, many of the horses swimming in the swift current, and, driven off the picket there, moved rapidly to the flank and rear of Capron, just south of Rally Hill, and, attacking with Ross's Brigade (except the 9$^{th}$ Texas), drove off the rear guard (7$^{th}$ Ohio Cavalry), under Capron in person, capturing one company and some wagons, the Federals retreating in confusion in the direction of Franklin. This left a force of four regiments (5$^{th}$ Iowa, 14$^{th}$ and 16$^{th}$ Illinois, and 8$^{th}$ Michigan) cut off at the ford, numbering 1,500 men. These were, under Maj. J. Morris Young, commanding the 5$^{th}$ Iowa Cavalry, immediately formed in the darkness and gallantly charged through Ross's little force of 576 men, escaping in the direction of Franklin. This movement permitted Buford to cross, and Forrest's whole command was on the morning of the 29$^{th}$ concentrated in the direction of Hurt's Crossroads, fourteen miles northeast of Columbia, at which point Wilson had likewise concentrated his own forces, now greatly augmented by reenforcement. This movement to eastward by Major General Wilson was suggested by himself to General Schofield after learning that Forrest was forcing the crossing of Duck River at the fords between Davis Ford and the Lewisburg Pike at Hardison's Mills and was pressing Colonel Capron's force at the latter point, the dispatch imparting the information concluding with the words: "I move everything there at once."

This was approved by General Schofield, who at 2 p.m. of the 28$^{th}$ had directed General Wilson to move at once to the Lewisburg and Franklin Pikes and ascertain and report as to the condition of affairs and movements of the enemy. However, at 5:20 p.m. of the same day General Schofield became aware that his left flank had been entirely uncovered, and wrote General Wilson that the Confederate cavalry was crossing the river very near the left of his infantry, and, fearing that the cavalry pickets had all been withdrawn, warned General Wilson that he should at once remedy that mistake.

Gen. Thomas J. Wood, commanding the 3$^{rd}$ Division, 4$^{th}$ Army Corps, and posted on the extreme left of General Schofield's line, fronting the Duck River crossing at Columbia, detected this mistake at once and wrote General Stanley that he was informed that the cavalry had all been withdrawn from that flank, and warning him that if the error was not corrected the infantry pickets would be helpless, and that the whole Confederate army might soon be over on that flank without hindrance.

General Wilson seems to have obtained the idea that General Forrest's objective point was Nashville via Franklin, and so firmly was he impressed with this idea that in retreating before the Confederate leader next day he rode entirely past the flank of Schofield's forces, retreating along the

Franklin Pike in the vicinity of Spring Hill, leaving that hapless commander entirely uncovered, as he reasoned, to keep Forrest off of Nashville. This error the Confederate cavalry commander joyfully took advantage of by turning his whole force, except a few regiments at Mount Carmel Church, westwardly five miles to Spring Hill without molestation from Wilson, where he rapidly invested and came near capturing the town before Stanley's advance arrived. But more of this hereafter. As before stated, General Schofield had on the night of the 27$^{th}$ withdrawn his entire army to the north bank of the Duck River, moving by the Hampshire Pike and the railroad bridge and ford, two miles below Columbia (northwest) on the river, and taking position with the 4$^{th}$ Army Corps on a ridge across the long tongue-shaped strip of land in the horseshoe bend of the river, one and a half miles north of the town.

General Cox had crossed two brigades of his division on the night of the 25$^{th}$ at the pontoon bridge opposite the town, which was then floated down to the railroad bridge, and intrenched them on a nearer ridge, eight hundred yards from the river, throwing out his pickets to the margin of the river, where they constructed strong rifle pits. This was to prevent the Confederates from forcing a passage in front of the town.

Henderson's Brigade, of Cox's Division, remained on the south side and crossed over with the 3$^{rd}$ Division of Stanley's (4$^{th}$) Army Corps on the night of the 27$^{th}$, while Ruger's Division, of the 23$^{rd}$ Army Corps, crossing on the 25$^{th}$, had fortified at the railroad bridge, constructing a strong bridgehead there. The movement across the river was designed to take

Wayside exhibit regarding the N. and D. Railroad, Spring Hill, TN. (Photo Lochlainn Seabrook)

place on the night of the 26$^{th}$, but was prevented by the rainfall, which was heavy and continuous that night. General Loring's skirmishers discovered the movement as early as 3 a.m. on the 28$^{th}$, and pushed on to the enemy's skirmish intrenchments, and by daylight the skirmishers of General Walthall's and Stevenson's Divisions occupied the town.

Stevenson's Division, except Watkins's Brigade, which was moved down the river to the railroad crossing, at once moved forward through the town to the river bank and engaged the enemy's skirmishers (Reilly's Brigade, Cox's Division, 23$^{rd}$ Army Corps) across the river in an animated combat, the Confederate advance being composed of the 3$^{rd}$ and 18$^{th}$ Tennessee Regiments, under Col. W. R. Butler, and the 60$^{th}$ North

Carolina, which was disposed on the river bank above so as to enfilade the enemy's intrenched skirmish line, and soon drove the outposts from the margin of the river back to some timber two hundred yards northward. Thus matters remained during the day.

Soon after midnight General Hood, who had made preparations for such a movement on the 27th, but was delayed by the sluggish movement of his pontoon train, had perfected his preparations for his startling movement on the enemy's rear, and by 3 a.m. of the 29th moved forward to Davis Ford, about three miles above Columbia, where the evening before he had laid a pontoon bridge under cover of Forrest's movement, which drove Wilson back from the fords on Duck River. General Cheatham's Corps led, with the divisions of Cleburne, Bate, and Brown in the order named, and followed by Stewart's Corps, with the divisions of Loring, Walthall, and French in the order named, and these in turn followed by Johnson's Division, of Lee's Corps, which had been detached for that purpose. All these troops had crossed the river by 7:30 a.m., and moved rapidly by a country highway, the Davis Ford and Spring Hill road, toward the latter town, thirteen miles in the rear of Schofield's position at Columbia.

Edmund W. Pettus.

General Lee was left in front of Columbia with Stevenson's and Clayton's Divisions and all the artillery of the army, except one battery to each corps, with orders to press the enemy vehemently, effect a crossing if possible, and be ready to attack Schofield's force as soon as General Hood had, by reaching his rear line of communication, compelled him to retire from his position at Columbia.

The flanking force was composed of seven fine divisions numbering 19,621 effective men, exclusive of officers and camp followers, and to this must be added Forrest's Cavalry Corps of 5,400 effectives, including officers and artillery.

General Lee immediately began to pound away at Schofield's forces in the bend of the river opposite Columbia (Cox's Division, 23rd A.C.) with his artillery. This, with the fire of the 20th Alabama Regiment, Col. J. M. Dedman, from the right flank, just upstream, soon cleared the immediate river bank of skirmishers, and a pontoon boat under Captain Ramsey, of the engineers, was run down a steep bank of the river to the water under a scorching fire of the enemy, and served as a ferry on which, by 4 p.m., three regiments of Pettus's Brigade were crossed and formed under cover of the river bank and protecting rifles of the 30th Alabama Regiment, Col. J. K.

Elliott, on the southern bank of the stream. This work was handsomely done under the immediate direction of General Stevenson.

This being accomplished, General Pettus charged the enemy's outposts under Reilly, and drove them back to their main line, several hundred yards northward. Reenforced soon after by the remainder of his regiments and Holtzclaw's Brigade, of Clayton's Division, General Pettus presented a strong front, under shelter of which a pontoon bridge was at once laid, over which General Lee was ready to cross his two divisions and press the enemy as soon as they should begin to retire.

This maneuver of General Lee seems to have deceived General Schofield into the belief that General Hood's main force was still in front of him during most of the day of the 29th.

On the day previous (28th) at 8:45 in the morning Schofield had telegraphed General [George H.] Thomas:

> My troops and material are all on the north side of Duck River; the withdrawal was completed at daylight this morning without serious difficulty. Cox holds the ford in front of Columbia and Ruger the railroad bridge, which I partially destroyed. Stanley is going into position a short distance in the rear of Cox. I think I can now stop Hood's advance by any line near this and meet in time any distant movement to turn my position. I regret extremely the necessity of withdrawing from Columbia, but believe it was absolute; I will explain fully in time. Reenforcements will have to march from Spring Hill or Thompson's Station. Supplies should be sent to Thompson's Station.

A quarter of an hour later he wrote:

> I am in doubt whether it is advisable, with reference to future operations, to hold this position or to retire to some point from which we can move offensively. Of course we cannot recross the river here. I could easily have held the bridgehead at the railroad; but it would have been useless, as we could not possibly advance from that point. Please give me your views and wishes.

In the afternoon he informed General Thomas:

> The enemy was crossing in force a short distance this side of the Lewisburg Pike at noon to-day, and had driven our cavalry back across the river and the pike at the same time. The force is reported to be infantry, but I do not regard it as very probable. Wilson has gone with his main force to learn the facts, and drive the enemy back if practicable.

By 4 p.m. General Schofield seems to have concluded that Hood might be bent on mischief toward his left flank, and dispatched General Thomas:

> If Hood advances on the Lewisburg and Franklin Pike, where do you propose

to fight him? I have all the force that is necessary here, and A. J. Smith's troops should be placed with reference to the proposed point of concentration.

At 4:30 p.m. General Wilson dispatched General Schofield by courier:

The enemy's cavalry have crossed the river on the roads leading to Spring Hill. You had better look out for that place. I am doing all I can to carry out your instructions; shall get my force together first. The enemy may turn in your rear between us.

George H. Thomas.

This was in response to General Schofield's order to him at 2:10 p.m. of the same day directing him (Wilson) to move over to the Lewisburg Pike and ascertain the movements of the enemy.

After this General Schofield late in the afternoon ordered his supply and ammunition trains to be parked north of Rutherford Creek, four miles north of Columbia, on the Franklin Pike, and General Stanley was directed to move his divisions and take such position on the pike as would best defend the line of Duck River.

About this time Gen. Thomas J. Wood wrote General Stanley from his position, one and a half miles north of Columbia and east of the pike:

It seems to me a little strange that General Schofield does not intimate what measures he proposes to adopt to protect ourselves and guard our trains, and still more strange that he does not intimate such measures at once, as the enemy, according to his own statement, has crossed the river in force. It is perfectly patent to my mind if the enemy has crossed in force that General Wilson will not be able to check him. It requires no oracle to predict the effect of the enemy's reaching the Franklin Pike in our rear. I would suggest that, in case there should be any decided advance on our left flank by the enemy, General Kimball's two brigades should be thrown on my left at once, for the position is open and extensive; that without it being closed we could not extricate our trains, possibly not ourselves.

General Cox also had by this time become restless, and notified General Schofield as to the insecurity of his position and the danger of the enemy's being able to force a passage in his front.

By 3:30 a.m. of November 29 General Thomas, at Nashville, becoming alarmed by the reports of the rapid advance of General Forrest's cavalry, dispatched to General Schofield, saying:

> I desire you to fall back from Columbia and take up your position at Franklin, leaving a sufficient force at Spring Hill to contest the enemy's progress until you are securely posted at Franklin.

At 3 a.m. (29th) General Wilson also, from Hurt's Crossroads, on the Lewisburg Pike, sent him a dispatch by courier in haste, notifying him that he had just learned from a Confederate prisoner that the Confederate infantry were expecting every moment to march, and were building three pontoon bridges above Huey's Mill, which they were expecting to complete by 11 p.m. (28th). The dispatch concluded:

> I think it very clear that they are aiming for Franklin, and that you ought to get to Spring Hill by 10 a.m. There may be no strong advance of the enemy's cavalry till the infantry have crossed, which will be between now and daylight. Get back to Franklin without delay.

This dispatch was received about daylight. It was then (8:20 a.m.) that General Schofield dispatched to General Thomas:

> General Wilson reports the infantry crossing above Huey's Mill, about five miles from this place (Duck River east of Columbia). I have sent an infantry reconnaissance to learn the fact. If it prove true, I will act according to your instructions.

But before sending this dispatch at 8 a.m. he directed General Stanley to move at once with two divisions (Wagner's and Kimball's) to Spring Hill, and hurried all the trains off to the same point from the park north of Rutherford Creek. At this same hour General Ruger was directed to leave a regiment to guard the river at the railroad crossing, two miles below Columbia, and march at once with his division to Spring Hill; but this order was countermanded at 8:45 A.M., before General Ruger could get off.

At ten o'clock General Schofield halted General Kimball's Division at Rutherford Creek and wrote General Stanley (10:45 am), who had marched on rapidly toward Spring Hill, as follows:

> Wood's reconnaissance shows a considerable force at least on this side of the river. I have halted Kimball's Division this side of the creek and put it in position. I will hold the enemy until dark, and then draw back. Select a good position at Spring Hill covering the approaches and send out parties to reconnoiter on all roads leading east and southeast. Try to communicate with Wilson on the Lewisburg Pike; tell him to cover Franklin and Spring Hill and try not to let the enemy get between us.

And immediately the special held orders of the day were issued as follows:

Headquarters Army of the Ohio, Spring Hill, Tenn., Nov. 29, 1864. Special Field Orders, No. 166, No. 1. The army will return to Franklin in the following order—viz: General Stanley, with Wagner's Division, will hold his position at Spring Hill until the army and trains have passed, and will act as rear guard from that point.

Colonel Stewart's Cavalry, and also Colonel Hammond's, if he be within reach, will cover the flank of the rear guard, and take its place under proper circumstances.

At dusk this evening General Cox will withdraw all save his picket line, with a strong support, and march direct for Franklin, unless he finds the enemy drives in his pickets, in which case he will halt in the works in the rear of his headquarters until the enemy is checked and the movement can be conducted without danger to the column in the rear.

General Wood will continue the movement of General Cox, withdrawing by his right and following toward Franklin.

General Kimball will follow General Wood in like manner.

Wayside exhibit, Spring Hill, TN. (Photo Lochlainn Seabrook)

General Ruger will hold position on the north bank of Rutherford's Creek until all the troops, including skirmishers, shall have passed, when he will retire as rear guard, passing General Wagner at Spring Hill.

The pickets along Duck River will be withdrawn at midnight and will march at once to join their commands, except those of General Wood's right, which will halt in General Stanley's works one hour.

General Ruger's troops at Ducktown will march at eleven o'clock, will move along the railroad, and join the division where the railroad strikes the pike.

The trains will move without delay to Franklin under such escort as General Stanley may think necessary. If the necessary escort diminish too much the force at Spring Hill, General Stanley will detail from one of his other divisions sufficient force for the rear guard from that point. By command of Major General Schofield. J. A. Campbell, Major and Assistant Adjutant General.

At 10:45 a.m. Capt. William J. Twining, of the engineers, wrote General Schofield:

Our skirmish line is now two miles from where I left you. One mile in front of us a column of infantry is moving up from Huey's Mill or some point in that vicinity. After I first saw them, they changed the direction of their column behind a hill, and I cannot tell whether they intend to advance or merely to hold us in check. Colonel Post will hold on here till further orders.

Patrick R. Cleburne.

In the meantime the column of General Hood was marching rapidly northward along a country road from three to four miles east of the Franklin and Columbia Pikes, his leading corps marching with two divisions (Cleburne's and Bate's) in column on the road and Brown's Division about four hundred yards eastward on the flank, so as to at once come into line of battle as a supporting line in rear if attacked. At times the columns would leave the road and move across the country, maintaining a northerly direction, so as to reach the Rally Hill and Spring Hill Turnpike near Rutherford Creek crossing. This was accomplished about 2:30 p.m., and General Hood, riding with General [Mark P.] Lowrey at the head of the leading brigade of Cleburne's Division, led the column across Rutherford Creek on the Rally Hill Pike. It is worthy of note that no enemy was seen other than a few cavalry stragglers on the entire march until the immediate vicinity of Spring Hill was reached.

During the day General Wilson had kept both General Schofield and General Thomas fully advised of General Forrest's movements. At 10 a.m. he dispatched to General Schofield, through his adjutant general:

The enemy is driving us back rapidly on this road (Lewisburg and Franklin Pike). We are now at Mount Carmel.

And at 12 noon:

The enemy have driven us beyond the Ridge Church. They have gotten possession of the Peytonsville and Bethesda roads, which makes it impossible for them to cross Harpeth farther up than Henderson's Ford. Some of the officers of the command think that Forrest has divided his forces, sending some up on the Davis Ford road; but there is no doubt he has gone to Nashville with his whole force. I will endeavor to cover Franklin as much as possible until you get there.

And again at 4:10 p.m., from a position four miles east of Franklin, he wrote:

The enemy, after having pressed my command back this side of Ridge Meetinghouse, has disappeared, I think, moving via Peytonsville toward Nashville. . . . I have heard heavy firing in your direction all day, and feel very solicitous for you. I hope that you will pass the Harpeth [River] to-night. I shall be concentrated again in two or three hours, so as to cover the Brentwood Pike, and be able to reach the Nolensville Pike by daylight; so that should Forrest succeed in reaching Nashville ahead of me, I shall be there very closely behind him.

And at 2 p.m. of the same day he wired General Thomas at Nashville:

My impression is that Forrest is aiming for Nashville via Triune and Nolensville. A part of his force may have cut into Spring Hill; heavy artillery firing heard in that direction since 11 a.m. You had better look out for Forrest at Nashville to-morrow noon; I'll be there before or very soon after he makes his appearance.

But General Forrest had skillfully eluded General Wilson at Mount Carmel Church, to which point he had driven him by 10 a.m. At the church, which lies on a crossroad or pike leading directly westward to Spring Hill, five miles distant, Forrest, after a strong attack, dismounted, on some rail defenses occupied by Col. D. E. Coon's Brigade, who vainly attempted to check the pressure on General Wilson's rear, dislodged Colonel Coon, and, detaching Ross's Brigade of about six hundred men to press the pursuit toward Franklin, turned abruptly to the westward before Wilson's rearguard had disappeared from view, as witnessed by the writer himself, and rode rapidly to Spring Hill. General Wilson was deceived by a flanking movement to his leftward a few minutes before into believing that Forrest had moved with his whole force via Peytonsville to Nashville, and so reported, while he himself retreated rapidly to a point four miles east of Franklin and threw out several brigades toward Triune to try to ascertain Forrest's supposed movements in that direction.

Forrest, after a rapid ride, reached the front of Spring Hill about noon, and, moving to the left (or southward), dismounted part of his command and prepared at once for offensive operations. Thus it will be seen that General Hood by 3 p.m. had appeared in front of Spring Hill with an army corps 9,000 strong and a corps of cavalry 5,400 strong, with a second army corps (Stewart's and Johnson's Divisions, of Lee's Corps) near by at the crossing of Rutherford Creek, in easy supporting distance.[17]

General Schofield's army was still in front of Columbia watching General Lee's maneuvers across the river, except Wagner's Division, 4th Army Corps, under Stanley in person, which had arrived at Spring Hill near noon, and Kimball's Division, 4th Army Corps, which had been halted on the hills south of Rutherford Creek, four miles north of Columbia, and placed in position facing eastward to cover first the movement of the trains and then the right flank of Schofield's army when it should begin to fall back. Schofield himself was just (3 p.m.) starting with Ruger's Division for Spring Hill.

(Photo Lochlainn Seabrook)

All the supply, hospital, and ordnance trains, except a few wagons with each division, and all the artillery except a limited number of guns, eight hundred wheeled vehicles in all, had by 4 p.m. marched to Spring Hill and were parked west of the town on the commons between the village and the depot, some half mile away. The flank movement was certainly successful thus far, and it only remained to reap the results. A reference to the map [at the front of this book] will show the relative positions of the several divisions of both armies at different hours during the day, and will fully illustrate the execution of Hood's rapid march to the rear of Schofield at Spring Hill.

As soon as Forrest had formed his dismounted troops in line eastward of and before the village he commenced pressing forward with characteristic vigor on the enemy's outlying forces. As his skirmishers moved toward the village, Armstrong's Brigade and part of Buford's Division moving on either side of the Mount Carmel road from the northeast and east and General Chalmers a little later approaching north of the Rally Hill road and crossing McCutcheon's Creek near the tollgate on that road, about a mile south of the village, the head of Wagner's Division, under the immediate command of Gen. D. S. Stanley, corps commander of the 4th Army Corps, came in view on the Columbia Pike.

Hearing from some scouts that a command of cavalry was approaching from the eastward, and also hearing the sound of firing in the vicinity of the town, that accomplished commander at once, with true soldierly instinct, moved Wagner's Division forward at a double-quick. Opdycke's Brigade, in advance, was marched through the town and rapidly deployed, fronting north and northeast and covering the Franklin Pike and the approaches around to the Mt. Carmel road. Brushing away the small cavalry command endeavoring to reach the railroad station to the northwest of Spring Hill from the latter direction, Opdycke then deployed his troops in open skirmish order, the 24th Wisconsin, 44th Illinois, 125th Illinois, and 73rd Illinois being deployed in the order named from the railroad station, one-half mile northwest of the village, in a curved line around to the Mount Carmel road.

Before Opdycke reached the town the only troops there were four companies of the 73rd Illinois under Captain Jones, deployed north of the town on the Franklin Pike to stop stragglers, and two hundred men of the 12th Tennessee [U.S.] under Lieutenant Colonel Hoefling, and the 103rd Ohio, detached as a headquarter train guard. The former were the troops which were being driven in northeast of the town when Opdycke arrived. Following Opdycke, Col. John Q. Lane's 1st Brigade, 2nd Division, 4th Army Corps, was double-quicked to the east of the town and, deploying rapidly as they ran, in line of battle, with the 28th Kentucky (Colonel Boone) thrown out as skirmishers, charged down the slope and up the hill east of the village and south of the Mount Carmel road, pushing back the 2nd Mississippi Cavalry under Colonel Dillon, of Armstrong's Brigade, from the ridge top, about one-half mile east of the town.

Nathan B. Forrest.

Colonel Lane then fell back to the slope of the hill on the outskirts of the town and formed line of battle there, and at once threw up defenses or rifle pits. Meanwhile Gen. L. P. Bradley's Brigade, arriving also in double-quick time, was deployed on a wooded eminence about one-half mile east of the pike and three-fourths of a mile south of the town, and one half mile or more detached from the right flank of Lane's Brigade. Here he formed line of battle and threw up rail defenses having his command aligned from right to left in the following manner: 65th Ohio, 15th Missouri, 51st Illinois, and 79th Illinois, while the 42nd Illinois was posted about one hundred and fifty yards to the right of, and refused at an angle of forty-five degrees from, the line of battle. The 64th Ohio was soon after deployed as skirmishers. The 26th Ohio had previously been aligned one-half mile southwest of Bradley's right, and parallel with the Columbia Pike, to guard the approaching wagon trains at a crossing of a country road there; and when Bradley was about to be outflanked, the 36th Illinois, detached from Opdycke's Brigade by General Wagner, was double-quicked to, and posted at a point about two hundred and fifty yards from the pike, a little to the northward and rearward of Bradley's right, to support a section of Battery B, Pennsylvania Artillery, placed there by General Stanley to cover the ground between Bradley's right and the Franklin Pike as it approached

Spring Hill.

These dispositions were just in time to prevent Forrest's closing in on the village and immense park of wagons and artillery, being the entire train and reserve artillery of Schofield's Army.

Wagner's fine division, thus skillfully interposed by Stanley, numbered 5,689 rank and file, Lane's Brigade consisting of 1,666 men and officers and the other two brigades numbering approximately 2,000 men each. [The Battle of Spring Hill map at the beginning of this book show both the Federal and Confederate formations.]

Whether it was the news of Hood's passage of Duck River, just received by him, or of the near approach of Forrest's Cavalry that electrified Stanley into such determined energy, the fact seems to be that he at once grasped the situation and made such prompt and skillful disposition of his forces as not only served to check Forrest (who, flushed with victory, having driven Wilson's great cavalry corps entirely away from Stanley's flank, was now pressing hotly on the latter), but impressed, a few hours later, both Hood and Cheatham with the idea that there was a large force, not less than an army corps, in their front, as we shall see hereafter.

Forrest had detached General Ross's Brigade, of Jackson's Division, at Mount Carmel to follow Wilson several miles, and then turn in toward the railroad at Thompson's Station, three miles north of Spring Hill. This was accomplished by Ross, who, after burning several wagons en route there, and failing to capture the train of cars and engine, which got safely under the guns of a blockhouse at the station, moved south just before dark toward the east of Spring Hill in order to communicate with his division commander. This was the force which gave the alarm to Opdycke's men about sundown on the Franklin Pike.

After Lane's charge, which dislodged Dillon's $2^{nd}$ Mississippi Regiment from the hill one-half mile east of the village, most of the Confederate cavalry in that vicinity moved southward, and were concentrated in the vicinity of the tollgate and Dr. [George B.] Peters's residence just eastward of Bradley's position. General Forrest, with a detachment of Col. Alexander Chalmers's Regiment, rode to the hill southwest of the tollgate, over which Cleburne subsequently moved, and, carefully inspecting the ground and the turnpike along which the Federal trains were then moving, ordered General Chalmers to take Wilson's Regiment, of Buford's Division, and charge the position of Bradley, thinking it contained only a cavalry detachment. General [James R.] Chalmers promptly obeying, after telling General Forrest that he believed the rail defenses were occupied by infantry, which Forrest refused to believe, charged with his escort and Wilson's Regiment (mounted) on the rail piles, and was quickly and sharply repulsed by Bradley's men, which caused Forrest laughingly to remark in his quaint way: "They was in there sure enough, wasn't they, Chalmers?"[18]

James R. Chalmers.

After this there was pretty constant skirmishing along the entire east front for half an hour, when Cleburne's Infantry arrived in the vicinity of the tollgate and formed line of battle. About 2:30 p.m. the 64th Ohio, detached as skirmishers, moved forward and reached the vicinity of Dr. Peters's residence, east of the tollgate, but was there assailed by dismounted cavalry of Chalmers's and Buford's command and hastily driven back on Bradley's position, whence they were sent to the rear of his right flank to support the 42nd Illinois in that quarter.[19]

General Hood, riding with Lowrey's Brigade at the head of his column, reached Rutherford Creek about 3 p.m., as before stated. Quickly he pressed the crossing of the stream by Cleburne's Division, which he directed General Cheatham, commanding the corps, to send forward to the vicinity of the tollgate on the Rally Hill Pike and there form them and forward on the enemy. General Cheatham was further instructed to remain at the creek and urge forward the passage of Bate's Division and move it forward to support Cleburne.[20]

General Cleburne, halting his division of three brigades (one being absent) of a little more than three thousand men about midway between the tollgate and Captain Thompson's residence [Oaklawn], formed them *en echelon* fronting westward, Granbury on the left and Lowrey on the right, with Govan in the center, and about 4 p.m. moved forward (westward) toward the turnpike. At the same time General Forrest formed Bell's Brigade, of Buford's Division, on Cleburne's right to advance in line with him, this being the only one of his brigades with any ammunition left, and it had only four rounds. This movement of Cleburne's, and the direction of it, was ordered by General Hood in person, who had ridden to the front, General Cheatham being still at the creek pressing the crossing of Bate's Division.

General Bate's Division came up while the left of Cleburne's Division was passing out of view over a hill to the left of the Rally Hill road. General Bate's line was formed just south of Cleburne's position of formation, and when ready was directed to move westward by General Hood in person, General Cheatham not being then at hand.

In the meantime General Brown, reaching the creek (Rutherford's), to the right of Cleburne and Bate, moved westward to the point of common passage, and then, directed to move by a country road northward in the direction of Dr. Caldwell's house, and when near that place, to the northwestward, reached the Rally Hill Pike again near and a little north of the tollgate. He at once went into position fronting northward and at right angles to Cleburne's formation, but almost directly facing the town. From this point he moved forward about five hundred yards and halted with his right on the Rally Hill Pike in the bend of McCutcheon Creek, and his left extending westward to a point some six hundred yards east of Bradley's center, where it remained during the night without further movement.

Cleburne, moving forward in the alignment with Bell on his right, drove in the Federal skirmishers rapidly, and about fifteen minutes past four o'clock struck with his right brigade (Lowrey's) the right of Bradley's line behind its rail defenses on a slight elevation with woods in the front and rear.[21]

This he at once charged, Lowrey and Govan making a half wheel to the right, so as to conform to the right flank of Bradley, which, as we have seen, consisted of the 42nd Illinois and the 64th Ohio, separated about one hundred and fifty yards from Bradley's right, and refused from his line of battle at an angle of forty-five degrees. Bell's Brigade halted at the farm fence in the edge of the woods in front of Bradley, from which position he had driven the 64th Ohio skirmishers, and lay down behind the fence, firing heavily on Bradley's front. As Lowrey swung his left around, Govan conforming, they overlapped the right of the refused line and took it in reverse, which caused the whole right wing of Bradley's to crumble, involving not only the two regiments on the right but the 65th Ohio also; and as the eager Confederates pressed forward, the remaining regiments (the 15th Missouri and the 51st and 79th Illinois, the two last of which had not been attacked in front) also were driven back, and all except the 79th Illinois fled in disorder to the outskirts of the town, where they were rallied by Generals Stanley and Wagner under the cover of eighteen guns and again formed in line.[22]

John C. Brown.

The stubbornness of the 79th Illinois and a few other troops which fell back slowly from Bradley's left flank, deploying first behind a fence and then another, caused General Lowrey to fear that he would be assailed in flank, and he called General Cleburne's attention to the line, when that commander moved against them with Govan's Brigade and rapidly drove them back upon their main line, on an eminence across a small ravine south of town. Granbury, moving on Lowrey's left and swinging in conformity with his line, soon encountered the 36th Illinois and the two gun sections of Battery B, Pennsylvania Volunteers, placed on General Bradley's right rear, drove the regiment back on the guns, and then back to their main line, near the town.[23]

Moving after this charge rapidly by the right flank in column, General Granbury double-quicked his brigade about half a mile on Lowrey's and Govan's left, passing across the fire of the batteries on the pike near the town, and, being recalled by General Cleburne, moved back by the left flank and formed under cover of the farm fence almost in front of the first position of the two gun section and parallel with the pike, about two hundred yards distant, and remained there until after dark.

While this charge was being made Generals Stanley and Wagner, seeing that Bradley's Brigade would be driven back on the town, concentrated the artillery of four batteries—in all eighteen guns—near the pike at the outskirts of the village, and directed Colonel Lane to bring up his brigade in order that they might rally Bradley's men under cover of that command. Colonel Lane, at once changing front forward on his right battalion, double-quicked his men southward and westward, so as to reach the left front of Bradley's routed men, and formed line of battle facing Lowrey and Govan, throwing out a regiment and battalion (100th Illinois and one company, 40th Indiana) on his left, so as to threaten Cleburne's right flank, which caused him to halt and re-form his two brigades.

At this juncture General Cleburne's horse ("Red Pepper") was wounded by a shell. As soon as Cleburne's line was reformed and ready to advance, Granbury on the pike and Govan and Lowrey on Bradley's and Lane's new position, Colonel Bostick, of General Cheatham's staff, appeared with an order from General Cheatham directing General Cleburne not to move forward, but to remain where he was until further orders. "But for the order brought by Colonel Bostick," remarked Adjutant General Mangrum, of Cleburne's staff, "Cleburne would have been on the pike and had possession of Spring Hill in less than ten minutes."

It was now near sunset, and General Cleburne remained in line of battle until nightfall, and then went into bivouac. Granbury's Brigade being withdrawn about two hundred yards and formed on his left, the line of the brigade being refused, so as to conform to the direction of the Columbia and Franklin Pike.

General Bate, moving westward by direction of General Hood with orders to reach the pike and swing around thence toward Columbia, moved forward in line of battle more than a mile, and, finding from the sound of firing at Cleburne's front, on his right, that that officer had changed direction, also changed his direction slightly to the right. After getting a guide and learning of the exact course of the turnpike, changing again to the right, he came into the pike to the north of Col. Nat Cheairs's residence [Rippavilla], and, finding the 26th Ohio Regiment there, attacked it with his sharpshooters under Major Caswell, followed by his whole division, and was rapidly driving them across the pike when he was overtaken by an order from General Cheatham through Lieutenant Schell to change direction to the rightward and ascertain and form on General Cleburne's left.

This he did, moving northeastward; and after ascertaining the left flank of Granbury's Brigade, which was refused, so as to protect Cleburne's flank from attack in the direction of the Columbia and Franklin Pike, he formed, fronting northward with his left brigade in turn thrown back to protect his flank from the Federals passing along the pike toward Spring Hill, and went into bivouac for the night. General Johnson's Division, of Lee's Corps, temporarily attached to Cheatham's Corps, was moved westward from the Rutherford Creek crossing and formed fronting the Columbia and Franklin Pike in extension of Bate's left brigade.

Columbia Pike (Highway 31), also the Columbia-Franklin Pike, as it looks today heading south into Spring Hill, TN. (Photo Lochlainn Seabrook)

Up to and including the operations above described there is no dispute as to the movements, nor is it alleged that there was any failure on the part of any commander to execute his orders promptly and efficiently on the side of the Confederates. But from this time on the matter has heretofore been involved in much doubt and uncertainty, and numberless articles have been written by persons more or less well informed as to the causes which led to the failures on the part of the several Confederate subordinate commanders to take advantage of the desperate situation of the Federal forces, not only those of Wagner's Division guarding the immense reserve artillery, ordnance and supply train in the village, but the main body under Schofield as well.

. . . Opdycke's Brigade still stood on the extended skirmish line north of the town and more than a mile in the rear of Bradley's and Lane's new positions. Those commanders, as before seen, had re-formed their brigades south of the village on a line extending from a point west of the Franklin Pike for half a brigade front to a point somewhat west of the Rally Hill Pike as it entered the town, the two pikes approaching each other as they neared the village until at the Federal line they were not much more than half a mile apart. Lane's movement to save Bradley had entirely uncovered, except by his skirmishers, the town to the eastward from Opdycke's right to his (Lane's) new line southward, a space of about three-fourths of a mile. Confronting Bradley and Lane on the southward and about seven hundred yards distant were Cleburne's and Brown's Divisions in battle formation, numbering fully 6,785 men (our brigade absent), and curiously enough the same two divisions which next day at Franklin ran over the same two brigades in the center line of the Federal works, almost without firing a gun until they had reached the latter's intrenchments or rifle pits.

Road named after Patrick R. Cleburne, Spring Hill, TN. (Photo Lochlainn Seabrook)

Southwest of these two divisions and in easy supporting distance was Bate's Division, 2,100 strong, just approaching and firing into the Federals on the Franklin Pike. To the east was Forrest's whole force except one brigade (Ross's, of Jackson's Division), say 5,000 dismounted men, fronting the line abandoned by Lane when he went to the support of Bradley; and to the southeastward, about two miles, at Rutherford Creek, lay Stewart's Corps and Johnson's Division, of Lee's Corps, say 10,700 men in line of battle, fronting westward toward the Columbia and Franklin Pike. The total Confederate effective force present on the field was 25,021.

Schofield's main force, except Ruger's Division, en route to Spring Hill, and yet fully six miles away, was in battle formation from Rutherford Creek to Duck River, from eight to ten miles south of Spring Hill, where it remained until 6 p.m.

From this hour the true occurrences of the fateful afternoon and night must be gathered from the narratives of not only Generals Cheatham, Brown, Bate, Lowrey, Stewart, and others published years ago in the *Courier-Journal* as part of General Cheatham's defense, but also from the additional narratives of a number of other well-informed and in some cases distinguished persons collected by the author and now for the first time printed.

It is to be hoped that the narrative will elucidate the mystery that has so long hung over the occurrences of the afternoon and night of the 29th of November and leave little for further investigation by the future historian.

At about 5 p.m., when Cleburne had re-formed his line after the attack on and overthrow of Bradley's Brigade and had connected on his right with General Brown's Division, there were three courses still open to General Hood—viz.:

1. To push Brown and Cleburne forward on Spring Hill with the energy, if necessary, displayed by those commanders next day at Franklin, on which occasion they charged over the same two brigades, now confronting them at Spring Hill, without faltering, and drive Wagner's Division, in its scattered condition, from the town, taking possession of the great [Union] wagon park, and to follow the movement by leaving Forrest to look after them, while Cheatham's three divisions changed front to the rear, confronting Schofield as he approached, and Stewart and Johnson should stand ready to strike him in flank next morning, while Lee, with his two remaining divisions, pressed him in the rear. Such a movement would likely have resulted in the destruction of Schofield's command, though a hot battle would probably have ensued.

2. Another course would have been to have thrown Cleburne or Bate across the pike south of Spring Hill in front of Schofield, while Stewart and Johnson were pressed forward on his right flank and Brown's Division was interposed to prevent Stanley giving succor to his chief, which he most certainly would have endeavored to do, notwithstanding the necessity of guarding the trains committed to the charge. This movement would have scattered Hood's command more than in the first case and left a powerful division of the enemy, 5,600 strong, in an embarrassing position on his right flank.

3. Still another course would have been to have moved Stewart northward to the east of Spring Hill, reaching the pike, say, a mile north of the village, his line extending south to about the right of Brown's Division, while Brown, Cleburne, Bate, and Johnson were deployed along and facing the pike to the southward of Spring Hill, ready to attack when Schofield moved up to the village.

This plan might have accomplished the desired purpose, but would have resulted probably in a junction of Schofield's and Stanley's forces, and given Schofield access to his wagons, ammunition trains, and artillery, without which he could have maintained himself but for a short time.

The facts seem to show that Hood actually attempted each of these maneuvers in turn, and failed in all of them.

The reasons for their failures will now be

William B. Bate.

inquired about so far as the information at hand can he made to develop them.

Beginning at five o'clock, after Cleburne's successful initial attack, General Cheatham's statement will be quoted first from his narrative above referred to, and then General Brown's and other officers in connection with the failure of Cleburne and Brown to carry out the first plan of attack agreed upon by Generals Hood and Cheatham—viz.: To move their divisions directly forward on Lane's and Bradley's Brigades, in front of the village on the south, and drive Wagner from the town.

General Cheatham says, quoting only such parts of the narrative as relate to the attack of Cleburne and Brown:

> Shortly after Bate's Division had disappeared over the same range of hills I heard firing toward Cleburne's right, and just then General Brown's Division had come up. I thereupon ordered Brown to proceed to the right, turn the range of hills over which Cleburne and Bate had crossed, and to form line of battle and to attack to the right of Cleburne. . . . After Brown had reached the position indicated to him and had formed line of battle, he sent to inform me that it would be certain disaster for him to attack, as the enemy's line extended beyond his right several hundred yards. I sent him word to throw back his right brigade and make the attack. I had already sent couriers after General Bate to bring him back and direct him to join Cleburne's left. Going to the right of my line, I found Generals Brown and Cleburne, and the latter reported that he had re-formed his division. I then gave orders to Brown and Cleburne that as soon as they could connect their lines they should attack the enemy, who were then in sight, informing them at the same time that General Hood had just told me that General Stewart's column was close at hand and that General Stewart had been ordered to go to my right and place his command across the pike. I furthermore said to them that I would go myself and see that General Bate was placed in position to connect with them, and immediately rode to the left of the line for that purpose.

In an article on the campaign published in the *New York Evangelist* of May 2, 1889, over the name of Henry M. Field, there is quoted from a letter written by Maj. Joseph Vaulx, of the staff of General Cheatham, the following narrative relative to the occasions here noted. It will be observed, however, that the statement of Major Vaulx, though written several years later, does not in some material respects agree with the statements of either General Cheatham or General Brown. Major Vaulx is quoted as saying:

> Cheatham's Corps was in advance on the march. As it approached Spring Hill he was ordered by General Hood to form it in line of battle in front of the Federal army, which was already in position, an order which he promptly obeyed, forming it from left to right as each division came up—Bate on the left, Cleburne in the center, and John C. Brown (who commanded Cheatham's old division) on the right. As Brown was the last to arrive, Cheatham pointed out his place to the right of Cleburne, and then gave his

orders, as soon as his division was formed in two lines, to move his right brigade forward and attack the Federals, who were posted south and west of Spring Hill, with their line curved around on the east side of the town. The map [at the front of this book] will show the exact position of both sides.

Cheatham told Brown that he would order Cleburne to attack on hearing his guns, and that as soon as Cleburne became engaged he would order Bate also to advance. With this Cheatham turned and rode back to give the order to Bate, expecting every moment to hear the signal from behind that the battle was begun, and kept asking impatiently: "Why don't we hear Brown's guns?" The reason was soon explained.

While Brown was forming his division General Strahl, who commanded his right brigade, reported to him that he had discovered a line of Federal infantry on a wooded hill in such a position that the moment he [Strahl] swung forward to the attack we would be exposed to fire on both the flank and in the rear. On hearing this Brown went to Strahl, who pointed out to him the position of the Federal line, and, seeing it, sent two staff officers to report the situation to Cheatham, who, not hearing the guns, had said to his staff: "Let us go and see what is the matter." On the way to Brown he met the officer who was coming to report the situation on the right, and, hearing it, said, "Go with me and report to General Hood just what you have said to me," which, being done, General Hood replied to General Cheatham: "If that is the case, do not attack, but order your troops to hold the position they are in for the night."

As to the events narrated in these recollections of General Cheatham and Major Vaulx the statement of General Brown, published together with General Cheatham's narrative, is now quoted literally.

After describing his arrival with his division on the Rally Hill Pike just north of the tollgate and near the outskirts of Spring Hill, General Brown says:

This was within an hour or an hour and a half of sunset. I could distinctly see the enemy in force, both of infantry and artillery, at Spring Hill; but did not, and perhaps could not at that point, see either troops or wagons moving on the Columbia Pike. Forrest's Cavalry were on higher ground northeast of my position. I was ordered to form line of battle and take Spring Hill. Gist's Brigade and the detachment from Strahl had not reported. I formed my line as speedily as worn troops could move, and after throwing forward a skirmish line advanced four or five hundred yards, when I discovered a line of the enemy thrown out of Spring Hill across and threatening my right flank, and I then discovered for the first time that General Forrest's Cavalry, which I had been assured would protect my right, had been ordered to another part of the field, leaving me without any protection on my

White Hall, Spring Hill, TN. Forrest and his men breakfasted here on the morning of November 29, 1864. (Photo Lochlainn Seabrook)

right flank or support in the rear. I had neither artillery nor cavalry, and was left in a position where I must meet with inevitable disaster if I advanced on Spring Hill. A hasty consultation with my brigade commanders resulted in a determination to suspend the advance and confer with the corps commander. I need not remind you that in a very few minutes you were upon the field and fully approved of what had been done, as also did General Hood a little later, when he directed that the attack should be delayed until the arrival of Generals Stewart and Gist, and in the meantime that the whole command should be held under orders to advance at a moment's notice. General Gist's Brigade reported a little after nightfall, and was immediately placed in position on my right. General Stewart's Corps came up later and went into bivouac on the stream in the rear of my right, where it remained until the following morning. I received no further orders that evening or during the night to advance or change my position.

The Spring Hill battlefield in June 2018. (Photo Lochlainn Seabrook)

Here is a distinct contradiction. General Cheatham declares that, after receiving word from General Brown that he was outflanked and giving him orders to throw back his right brigade and attack anyway, he rode in person to Brown's right, where he met Cleburne and Brown in person and told them to connect their lines, and as soon as this could be accomplished to attack, and that he would go personally and find Bate and bring him up to their support, and at once rode off for that purpose.

General Brown, on the other hand, says that at the interview mentioned both General Cheatham and General Hood, who was present, directed him to remain in line, but not to attack until Gist arrived and Stewart moved up on the flank. Which was in error? That is the important inquiry; for here was not only the turning point of the battle, but of the campaign as well, an hour pregnant with the most fateful consequences to a nation.

General Cheatham believed that he had given the orders to Brown to attack, and the sound of his guns was to be the signal for Cleburne to move forward. If he was mistaken, why did he ride after Bate to bring him to Brown's aid? Why did he ask repeatedly during the ride: "Why don't we hear Brown's guns?" Why did not Cleburne, that ever-alert commander, attack on Brown's left unless he was waiting for Brown's guns to give the signal?

There were one or two incidents which occurred just before dark while General Cheatham was gone which seem to give color to General Brown's statement that he had no orders, or at least to show that he declared to several persons during that late hour that he was without orders.

General Chalmers relates that while General Brown's Division was standing idly facing the town he rode down to General Brown's position and, addressing the General, asked him why he did not advance and attack. "General Brown," relates General Chalmers, "with whom I was on most excellent terms and who was notably a most agreeable man in his manners, answered me, as I thought, very curtly, saying: 'I have no orders.' His tone somewhat nettled me, and I replied in much the same tone to him: 'General, when I was circumstanced as you are at Shiloh, I attacked without orders.' Saying this, I rode off, and did not see him again during the afternoon."

In a letter written subsequently to the writer General Chalmers states:

> I remember very distinctly seeing Gen. John C. Brown at Spring Hill on the evening of the day before the battle of Franklin. I cannot say exactly where it was, as I was then and am now unfamiliar with the locality. I know it was near a house on a hill from which could be seen the retreating wagon trains of the Federals moving rapidly along the pike toward Nashville. I rode up to him and pointed to the retreating enemy, and told him I could pilot him to where he could cut off their retreat. He replied that he had no orders to attack the enemy. I replied to him that at Shiloh I had attacked the enemy without orders, and won compliments by it, and he could do the same. He replied: "I would prefer to wait for orders." I do not remember the exact hour of the evening, but there was time enough to have struck a decisive blow to the enemy, in my opinion.

It is also related by Capt. H. M. Neely, then assistant adjutant general of Carter's Brigade, in Brown's Division, that the failure of the division commander to attack was a subject of much comment along the line while the command was waiting in line of battle across the Rally Hill Pike. Captain Neely says:

> Late in the afternoon, when General Brown had remained quietly in his position in front of Spring Hill for a long time, with the enemy in full view and at a short distance, Maj. John Ingram and I, having nothing else to do, rode out as far to the front as we could prudently to look the field over and

find out what was going on. We could plainly see the enemy passing along the Spring Hill Pike, and there seemed to be a great amount of hurry and confusion in their movements. They did not appear to be in large force, and doubtless fully understood their perilous situation. We turned about, and on reaching Brown's line met General Carter, who was lying down under a tree, and asked if he knew why an attack was not made, and he replied: "No; I am not in command." A little farther to the rear we met General Brown, and told him of what we had seen and our impressions of the situation in our front, and put the same question to him, and his reply was: "I don't know; I have no orders." We then told him in a pleasant way that if he would take the responsibility of beginning the attack without orders he could safely count on a "new feather in his cap," as it would be a quick and easy matter to capture or destroy Schofield's Corps in its present condition. At that he laughed and said: "No; I must wait for orders." I am not able to state the precise time when the conversation with General Brown took place, but the day was nearly spent. A little later darkness came on, and the troops were ordered in bivouac for the night.

The writer has also obtained the following statements, throwing new light on these events. The Right Reverend Bishop Ellison Capers, of South Carolina, then Col. Ellison Capers, who commanded the 24th South Carolina Regiment in Gist's Brigade, says in a letter to the author:

I was colonel commanding the 24th South Carolina Volunteers, Gist's Brigade, Cheatham's Division, Hardee's Corps. General Cheatham was commanding the corps and Gen. John C. Brown was commanding our division. The points of special importance in your letter of inquiry refer to the time when we were in position ready to attack at Spring Hill and the extent of the Federal line of battle in our front, and particularly as to its extent on our right flank. The other inquiry as to what transpired at division headquarters, etc., I knew nothing whatever. I give you the extent of my knowledge and recollections. Sorry I cannot now refresh my memory by a reference to my notes taken at the time and sent by me to the War Department Record Office. We (Cheatham's Division) were in position immediately in front of Spring Hill and in line of battle parallel with the road on which the Federal forces were forming, moving, and in great confusion, in full time to make the attack before dusk. My own regiment was ready to move, and so was Gist's Brigade, by a few moments after sundown. We were in momentary expectation of moving and in full view of the confusion at Spring Hill. We could not understand why we did not attack, and every man felt and I heard hundreds remark that for some cause we were losing a grand opportunity. About dusk General Gist (and I think General Strahl) and I, with several staff officers, rode out on our brigade right and up the hill toward the Federal line. They were pulling down fences and tearing off plank from houses and evidently putting their men in position in our front and on our right, but we

Ellison Capers.

could not see distinctly. We heard their commands and the tramp of the horses and men and the rumble and rattle of wheels most distinctly; indeed, we were so near that as I turned to ride off I emptied my pistol at the sound of voices in our front.

Now as to the extent of the Federal line on our right: I am confident that when we were first formed for attack before dusk their line did not overlap ours. This was precisely what we felt—viz., that we could take the road on their left (our right) and block their way. As dark came on we could hear them moving to our right. When it was light enough to see, I could see no troops on the Franklin side of Spring Hill; but we heard firing on our extreme right, which we understood at the time was Forrest engaging the Federal cavalry. This is really the extent of my knowledge and recollection. I believed at the time, and I have been satisfied in my mind ever since, that we lost a grand chance at Spring Hill. I am as sure as we can be of anything which was yet to be tried that an attack at Spring Hill like that Cheatham made at Franklin the next afternoon would have given us an easy victory and the possession of General Schofield's line of retreat. He was an able general, and commanded veterans; and the defense he made at Franklin showed that an easy victory, no matter what the force of the attack, was not then for Hood. But at Spring Hill the line was being formed (whatever its strength) when we were ready to assail it. It was in confusion and on a retreat, and did not extend beyond our right.

From a brother of a deceased staff officer then with the staff of Cheatham's old division this statement, preserved in the family annals, has been obtained. It is of much importance as showing how the failure to attack by Brown's Division was considered at division headquarters. The narrative says:

General Brown's Division was on the right of the Confederate line at Spring Hill on November 29, 1864. When the formation for the attack was complete, General Cheatham came to General Brown's position and asked him if he was ready to advance. General Brown replied that he was, and that his skirmishers were already thrown forward. General Cheatham then directed General Brown to advance and attack the Federal position with energy, saying: "I will go and direct the other commanders along the line to advance as soon as they hear your guns." General Cheatham then rode off with his staff to the left.

About this time the Federal commander threw out a regiment across General Brown's front which, in case of his advance, would overlap his right. General Brown hesitated in face of this new condition to advance. His staff officers (Cheatham's old division staff), or some of them, urged him to press forward and make the attack. General Brown replied that the responsibility of attacking a longer line and exposing his flank was a great one, and he did not care to assume it himself. He said that if General Cheatham were there he doubted if he would, under the changed condition of affairs, attack himself. Capt. John Ingram, who was present (and who had been drinking some), said: "General, if you will give me your escort company, I will drive that regiment away." General Brown replied: "You may consider yourself under arrest, Captain Ingram." General Brown, being again urged to attack, said he would go and overtake General Cheatham and report to him the present situation. Before General Cheatham was found it was dark and too late to move.

The Federal regiment referred to was, as heretofore stated, the 100th Illinois and Company F, 40th Indiana, thrown out by Col. John Q. Lane to the left of his brigade at the end of Cleburne's charge to threaten Cleburne's flank. Of this maneuver Colonel Lane says in his report:

> I moved the 100th Illinois and Company F, 40th Indiana, to my left, so as to hit the enemy in flank, which caused him to stop and re-form his lines. Before he could again advance, the darkness of night made our position secure.

Spring Hill battle site. (Photo Lochlainn Seabrook)

There were no other Federal troops in front of Brown's center and right during the afternoon. Those at whom Colonel Capers fired his pistol after dark were troops placed at the edge of the village after night by General Schofield to protect the flank of his retreating column along the pike, and who were endeavoring to barricade themselves.

There are few other sources of information remaining to be derived from men who are likely to be informed reliably as to the occurrences of this evening, as relates to Brown and Cleburne's failure to attack before dark. Cleburne was killed next day at Franklin, as were also Gist, Strahl, and John C. Carter, brigade commanders in Brown's Division; while Gen. G. W. Gordon, the surviving brigade commander, was captured and made no report. General Gordon is still living, but has, he states, no personal knowledge of these matters. General Brown wrote out a statement of these matters before his death. It is not accessible to the public, nor is it known what light, if any, it would throw on the occurrences of the fateful evening if published. A few staff officers who might be able to elucidate much that is mysterious about the matter still survive; but if such knowledge exists in their minds, they have thus far declined to disclose any part of it to the world.

Two other statements will be quoted as bearing on the issue. Gen. A. P. Stewart relates that on the early afternoon of the 30th, the day succeeding these occurrences,

General Hood complained to me that General Cheatham would not obey his orders to attack, and said that he had sent staff officer after staff officer to him to urge him on, and finally sent Governor Harris. I did not say it, but it was on my tongue to say that "You, General, ought to have taken command yourself and made the attack."

The other statement is by Major Vaulx, who says:

Isham G. Harris.

As we were on the march to Franklin I was riding by General Brown, and he said to me: "General Hood is mad about the enemy getting away last night, and he is going to charge the blame of it on somebody. He is as wrathy as a rattlesnake this morning, striking at everything. As he passed along to the front a while ago he rode up to me and said: 'General Brown, in the movement to-day I wish you to bear in mind this military principle: that when a pursuing army comes up with the retreating enemy he must be immediately attacked. If you have a brigade in front as advance guard, order its commander to attack as soon as he comes up with him. If you have a regiment in advance and it comes up with the enemy, give the colonel orders to attack him; if there is but a company in advance, and if it overtakes the entire Yankee army, order the captain to attack it forthwith; and if anything blocks the road in front of you to-day, don't stop a minute, but turn out into the fields or woods and move on to the front.'"

The writer is fully conscious of the fact that the voices of the principal actors in that eventful drama are stilled in death, and that it is not permissible to even the earnest historian to wander in the fields of surmise and conjecture as to those motives and secrets which they have chosen to carry with them unuttered to the grave. Only from what is disclosed can we legitimately draw conclusions that are just both to the actors and to the truth of history.

All the foregoing statements taken together clearly establish that General Cheatham was correct in his recollections, and that he did order Brown and Cleburne to attack Spring Hill as soon as they could connect their lines after Cleburne had re-formed his division and drive the force in front of them (Lane's and Bradley's little brigades, as it turned out) through the town. And it may be safely assumed from Major Vaulx's statement that the sound of Brown's guns was to be the signal for Cleburne to begin the attack in his quarter of the field. Such an attack would have given us [the Confederates] the town in thirty minutes.

The incident mentioned by Major Vaulx of Strahl seeing the enemy on his right and pointing them out to Brown and of Brown sending the staff officer to Cheatham, then returning from his quest of Bate, and of Cheatham going with the staff officer to Hood, who replied, "If that is the case, do not attack, but hold your troops in the position they are in for the night," is apparently a confusion of time and incidents. For it is perfectly clear that after General Brown first notified General Cheatham that he was outflanked and was ordered in turn to throw back his right brigade and attack, that General Cheatham, riding to Brown's position, there met Brown and Cleburne, and in pursuance of urgent orders from Hood directed them to attack as soon as they could connect their lines, and then rode off to find Bate.

And it is further evident that after giving this order Cheatham did not see General Hood again until, after returning from his ride to Bate's position, he went down to Hood's headquarters at the Thompson House [Oaklawn], all of which General Cheatham tells us himself, and adds:

> I was never more astonished than when General Hood informed me that he had concluded to postpone the attack till daylight. The road was still open—orders to remain quiet until morning and nothing to prevent the enemy from marching to Franklin.

If General Cheatham was astonished at this late hour at hearing such a statement from General Hood, it is not possible that he received such instructions from General Hood earlier in the afternoon before darkness had fallen and while he was on his way to the front to learn why Brown did not obey his order to begin the attack and give the signal to Cleburne by opening with his guns on the enemy.

What could have been General Brown's motive in delaying the attack after receiving explicit orders? Was he waiting for his remaining brigade (Gist's)? Col. Ellison Capers, of the 24th South Carolina Regiment in that brigade, says in his report that the brigade arrived and took position at sundown about the time Cleburne re-formed his line and Brown was ordered to attack, and in his narrative quoted above says, "in full time to make the attack before dark," and waited impatiently for orders to attack.

Was he waiting for General Stewart to move up an army corps and take position on his right flank to enable him to drive a brigade of the enemy from his front? Such a suggestion is in itself preposterous. Or did he (General Brown) in any way misunderstand his orders as to the nature of attack to be made? This cannot be, for he tells us himself that he had no orders.

General Brown was a man of great energy and force of character, was possessed of strong military acumen and splendid courage. He said once playfully in the writer's presence during the Georgia campaign that he was "made a sort of military convenience in the Army of Tennessee, and was shifted around by the commanding general into all the hard places."

When General Cheatham was promoted to the command of Hood's Corps and afterwards of Hardee's Corps, General Brown was appointed to command that officer's fighting division, a most complimentary assignment in itself. The true reasons for this inexplicable failure on General Brown's part to obey the orders which General Cheatham declares he gave will perhaps never be ascertained unless indeed his unpublished statement should be given to the public and should contain the long-sought explanation. General Brown's reasons, so far as he gave them in his lifetime, are, as already quoted from the article in the *Courier-Journal*:

> I had neither artillery nor cavalry, and I was left in a position where I must meet with inevitable disaster if I advanced on Spring Hill. A hasty consultation with my brigade commanders resulted in a determination to suspend the advance and confer with the corps commander. I need not remind you that in a very few minutes you were upon the field and fully approved of what had been done, as also did General Hood a little later when he directed that the attack should be delayed until the arrival of Generals Strahl and Gist, and in the meantime that the whole command should be held under orders to advance at a moment's notice. General Gist's Brigade reported a little after nightfall, and was immediately placed in position on my right. General Stewart's Corps came up later and went into bivouac on the stream in the rear of my right, where it remained until the following morning. I received no further orders that evening or during the night to advance or change my position.

The Absalom Thompson House, Oaklawn, Spring Hill, TN. Headquarters of John Bell Hood, November 29, 1864. (Photo Lochlainn Seabrook)

This statement is very direct and shows that General Brown did not seem to understand that he had been peremptorily ordered to attack the enemy, as General Cheatham declares, and the staff understood, and this is given color by his statements to Cheatham, Neely, and others on the field, as quoted above. Such things sometimes occur on the battlefield, and misapprehension of orders often leads to fatal consequences.

But however that may be, with the coming of darkness the opportunity passed for the certain destruction of Schofield's army, and next day on the bloody field of Franklin that army paid the fearful penalty for the mistake, whose ever it was, a penalty which broke the spirit of the proud Army of Tennessee and forever destroyed all hope of Confederate success in the West.

The term "certain destruction" above is used advisedly, for there were, as before stated, two other courses open to General Hood, and which he attempted to carry into effect. The second of these courses was still open when darkness came, and that was to occupy the Columbia Turnpike south of Spring Hill. There is considerable mystery enveloping these operations also and their fated miscarriage, but not so much as pertained to Brown's and Cleburne's movements.

When Cleburne was attacking with his light brigade the right flank of Bradley's men behind the rail defenses, General Granbury, as we have seen, moved forward on Cleburne's left straight toward the Franklin Pike, along which the Federal wagon train was still moving. When about three hundred yards of the turnpike, the brigade was halted and double-quicked by the right flank for about half a mile, passing northeastward and parallel with the pike and across the front of the battery on the outskirts of the town. The brigade was then moved back over the same ground and halted, facing the position abandoned by this battery about dark. After nightfall it was thrown forward to the farm fence, eighty or one hundred yards from the pike, and ordered to lie down behind the fence. Troops were soon heard moving on the pike, which proved afterwards to be the head of Ruger's Division, which had forced its way past Bate. Capt. R. T. English, adjutant general on the Staff of General Granbury, in doubt whether they were Bate's men, reported to be moving from that quarter, or Federal troops, passed through the fence to ascertain the nature of the movement, and was almost immediately captured by the Federal flankers, part of the 23rd Michigan Regiment, which had been deployed on the right flank of Ruger's Division as skirmishers, and which had, without knowing it, pressed up in the darkness to within a short distance of Granbury's line. Granbury had out no skirmishers in front of the fence, and the Federal column was thus enabled to pass unmolested along his front, while a number of Ruger's men strayed out in the darkness and got entangled in the Confederate lines and were captured. Why Granbury did not fire on this column or move forward across the pike and check its march will probably never be known, as that officer was killed next day in the assault on Franklin.

General Bate, as before related, formed on the left of Cleburne's formation, and when ready to move forward was directed by General Hood in person, General Cheatham not being present at the moment, to move directly westward to the pike and sweep toward Columbia. Moving forward, Jackson's Brigade on the right and Smith's Brigade in echelon on the front line, while Bullock's Brigade supported Smith, that officer approached the Franklin Pike to the right of Maj. N. F. Cheairs's residence [Rippavilla], about one and three-quarter miles southwestward of the village.

Benjamin F. Cheatham.

Major Caswell's Battalion of Sharpshooters, deployed as skirmishers, approached the pike about the point where the 26$^{th}$ Ohio Regiment had been posted to guard a country road running into the pike there and fired on that regiment, which at once retired with a loss of three killed and three wounded, and made its way to Spring Hill. It was just then that General Ruger's Division approached, and was in turn attacked by Bate's men. Strickland's 3$^{rd}$ Brigade, moving in advance with the 72$^{nd}$ Illinois, thrown out on the right flank as skirmishers, first encountered Bate's men less than one hundred yards distant, who fired on them. Moore's 2$^{nd}$ Brigade next pushed forward with the 23$^{rd}$ Michigan in advance and deployed as skirmishers on the right rear of Strickland's Brigade. All these troops were fired on by Bate's men, and lost lightly in wounded; but steadily kept pressing forward, passing in front of Granbury's Brigade, as above stated, when one-half a mile south of the village. A part of the wagon train was borne along the rear of this movement safely past the Confederate front.

It was while aligned in front of and firing on the pike with his skirmishers that General Bate received an order from General Cheatham through Lieutenant Schell to halt and move northward and form on Cleburne's left. Hesitating to obey this order, as he had received orders directly from the commander in chief, he soon received a second order from General Cheatham to the same effect, when he forthwith withdrew his line from contact with the enemy on the pike and moved northeastward, forming on Cleburne's left with some difficulty in the darkness and throwing back his left brigade to guard his flank from assault from the direction of the pike.

General Bate, after forming on Cleburne's left, went into bivouac, and soon after Johnson's Division, of Lee's Corps, was moved over to his left and rear and formed in line of battle, facing the pike and very near the position occupied by Bate when first assailing Ruger's advance on the pike.

The Federals thus were left free to move along the pike without further interruption, which they did, Ruger being followed by Whitaker's Brigade, of Kimball's Division, which was deployed parallel with the pike at the edge of the town, to guard that flank of the retreating army as it entered the village. These were followed in turn by Cox's, Wood's, and Kimball's Divisions, Cox reaching Spring Hill at about 11 p.m., Wood at 12 m., and Kimball about 1 a.m. on November 30.

The 12th and 16th Kentucky, left on picket at Columbia, came up just before day. General Stanley, in report, says of this approach to Spring Hill by Cox, Wood, and Kimball:

> So close were the enemy on our flank that when a column was not passing it was difficult for a staff officer or an orderly to get through on the road.

This was largely due not to any concerted movement, but to the enterprise of individual Confederates who went down on the pike to capture stragglers and get the contents of their haversacks.

Gen. Thomas J. Wood also reports of this movement into Spring Hill:

> The head of the 3rd Division (Wood's) arrived about midnight, passed rapidly and silently through the village, and took post about a mile north of it, formed parallel to the road and east of it. The object of this disposition was to cover the movement of the trains out of Spring Hill and toward Franklin. Cox's Division, of the 23rd Corps, had already moved on toward Franklin. As rapidly as possible the trains were drawn out of park and pushed toward Franklin. While this work was in progress the 1st Division (Kimball's) came up, pressed rapidly through Spring Hill, and moved on as a convoy to the trains. It was necessary to move the troops rapidly and silently through Spring Hill to avoid a night attack from an entire corps of four divisions (Cheatham's) which lay encamped within eight hundred yards of the road. The effect of a night attack on a column en route would have been beyond doubt most disastrous.

General Cheatham was evidently not aware of Hood's personal order to Bate "to reach the pike and sweep on toward Columbia," or he would not have ordered him to withdraw from the pike and march to the left flank of and in support of Cleburne. But for this order Bate, who had begun adjusting his lines to move on the pike with his whole force when he received the order, would have in ten minutes more struck Ruger squarely in the flank while on the march in the dark, and, if not with the disastrous results predicted by General Wood, with at least the result of stopping the Federal movement and compelling them to form line of battle and await the morning in his front.

Certainly no more trains or artillery could have passed his front during the night. In the meantime Gen. Edward Johnson's Division had, as we have seen, gone into bivouac about 10 p.m. on General Bate's left and facing the pike about four hundred yards distant from it and near where General Bate had first approached it in the afternoon. Of this command, General Cheatham, in his narrative, says:

> About eleven o'clock that night General Hood sent Major General Johnson, whose division had marched in the rear of Stewart's Corps, to report to me. I directed Major Bostick, of my staff, to place Johnson on my extreme left. A reference to the map [at the front of this book] will show the position of my corps and that of Johnson's Division during the night. About midnight Major Bostick returned and reported that he had been down to the turnpike and could hear straggling troops passing northward. While he was talking about this to Colonel Porter, my chief of staff, a courier from headquarters brought a note from Major Mason to the effect that General Hood had just learned that stragglers were passing along the road in front of my left, and "the commanding general says you had better order your picket line to fire on them."
>
> Before reading the note I ordered Major Bostick to return to General Johnson, whose command was on my left and nearest the pike, and say to him that he must take a brigade, or if necessary his whole division, and go onto the pike and cut off anything that might be passing. Major Bostick afterwards informed me that General Johnson commenced complaining bitterly at having been "loaned out," and asked why General Cheatham did not order one of his own divisions to go in; but at length ordered his own horse and rode with Major Bostick close up to the turnpike, where they found everything quiet and no one passing. General Johnson came with Major Bostick to my quarters and informed me of what they had done. It was about two o'clock in the morning of the 30th. This suggestion that I had better order my pickets to fire upon stragglers passing in front of my left was the only order, if that can be called an order, that I received from General Hood after leaving him at his quarters early in the night, when he informed me of his determination to wait until daylight to attack the enemy.

James H. Wilson.

Col. W. H. Sims, commanding the 10th and 44th Mississippi Battalion of Sharpshooters, in Sharp's Brigade, of Johnson's Division, thus writes of the occurrences of the night in front of Johnson's Division:

> My command did not reach the encampment near Spring Hill till ten o'clock at night. On my arrival I saw the twinkling camp fires of our army reaching northward far up the pike, stretching, as I was then told, about four miles. Our place of bivouac being assigned us, my command broke ranks and, being very tired, hastily sought their blankets for sleep. I had wrapped myself in my horse blanket, and was sinking into a much-needed slumber when I was aroused by the adjutant of our brigade with an order from General Sharp to get my troops immediately under arms, that our division (Johnson's) had orders to move perpendicularly upon the pike, and that General Cheatham

had orders to sweep down the pike at right angles to us. Our division was soon under arms in line of battle and the guns loaded. We waited hour after hour for the order to come to charge the enemy, who we understood were retreating along the pike four hundred yards in front of us toward Franklin. The next morning found us still in line waiting for the order to charge the pike, my own command having one by one sunk to sleep on the ground where they stood.

General Cheatham also quotes from a letter of Gov. Isham G. Harris to Gov. James D. Porter as follows to illustrate his position:

> General Hood on the march to Franklin spoke to me in the presence of Major Mason of the failure of General Cheatham to make the night attack at Spring Hill and censured him in severe terms for his disobedience of orders. Soon after this, being alone with Major Mason, the latter remarked that "General Cheatham was not to blame about the matter last night; I did not send him the order." I asked if he had communicated the fact to General Hood. He answered that he had not. I replied: "It is due General Cheatham that this explanation should be made." Thereupon Major Mason joined General Hood and gave him the information. Afterwards General Hood said to me that he had done injustice to General Cheatham, and requested me to inform him that he held him blameless for the failure at Spring Hill; and on the day following the battle of Franklin I was informed by General Hood that he had addressed a note to General Cheatham assuring him that he did not censure him with the failure to attack.

From the statement of General Cheatham's narrative that Major Bostick and General Johnson returned together and reported to him of having been to the Franklin Pike and found everything quiet about two o'clock in the morning of the 30th, it must have been after midnight when General Johnson and Major Bostick rode out to the pike to reconnoiter, and in all likelihood after the rear of Kimball's column, the last of Schofield's troops except the two regiments, 12th and 16th Kentucky, left on picket at Columbia, had passed by on the march into Spring Hill. Kimball's column reached Spring Hill about one o'clock in the morning, and must have passed Johnson's front nearly two miles south about 12:30 a.m., or earlier even than that, as all the Federal columns moved carefully, being in the immediate presence of the enemy. And General Cheatham says it was midnight when he received the note from Major Mason ordering him to fire on the Federal stragglers on the pike. One more opportunity was thus lost, which might, by the prompt movement of Johnson's Division on to the pike when he first began to go into bivouac, have checked the movement of Schofield's retreat and held him until daylight.

Of course Schofield might, if he had been attacked *en route* and found a column across his track, have moved northwestward toward the Carter's Creek Pike and reached Franklin in that way, but would have sacrificed his ordnance and supply train and perhaps Wagner's Division in so doing. This pike could have been reached by a country crossroad to the northwestward of Spring Hill, and this was the exact course General Forrest supposed Schofield was taking, as he related to General Stewart at his headquarters [Caldwell House] after dark.

The movement, however, does not seem to have occurred to General Schofield, as we shall later see.

The third and last course open to General Hood after his failure in the other two was to throw General Stewart's Corps northward to the eastward of Spring Hill, with his right across the Franklin Pike a mile beyond the village.

Whether the determination to do this was arrived at after General Hood learned that Bate had been withdrawn from the Columbia and Franklin Pike to Cleburne's left, or whether ordered to be done in conjunction with the movement he had directed Bate to make on the pike, is not clear. If, as General Cheatham recollects, he (Cheatham) on his return from the ride to the left in search of Bate was called to General Hood's quarters not long after dark and there told him of his disposition of Bate's force, it would seem that General Hood may have at once ordered Stewart to move north quickly and occupy with his right, or at least a division, the pike north of Spring Hill in order to accomplish what General Bate, through the inadvertent interruption of General Cheatham, had failed to do.

(Photo Lochlainn Seabrook)

On the other hand, it seems from General Stewart's report that he was halted in the execution of his order to seize and occupy the pike north of Spring Hill by reason of representations made by General Cheatham to General Hood before nine o'clock. However, General Stewart will be allowed, in addition to the matter contained in his report published in the *War Records*, to tell the story in his own language, which he has done in the following letter to the writer in April, 1895:

> After crossing Rutherford Creek about dusk November 29, 1864, I saw General Hood. He was almost or quite alone at a little fire in the edge of the woods to our left on the road. He said he wished me to move on and put my right across the turnpike road beyond Spring Hill, "your left," he said, "extending down this way" toward the creek. Said he: "The men have had a hard day's march, and I do not wish you to march your whole corps up to the right. It will be too far for the men to march." He gave me a guide, a young man of the neighborhood, who, he said, knew a road by which we could

move. I rode somewhat in advance of the troops, having the guide with me.

At a place where the road on which we were moving appeared to curve to the left—now some time after dark—there was a high gate on the right-hand side of the road. The guide said there used to be a road turning off from the one on which we were moving, through that gate which was the road we wished to find. I inquired if it would take us to the pike beyond Spring Hill. He said it would about a mile beyond, near the tollgate. "Then," said I, "that is the road we want." We rode through the gateway, the head of the column following, and soon passed a house on our left where some one informed me General Forrest was. I dismounted and went into the house to get such information as Forrest could give me. He said the enemy had left the direct road from Spring Hill to Franklin and taken the Carter's Creek Pike. I think it was just as I was mounting my horse to go on with the guide that the staff officer (whom I did not know) came up and said we were going wrong—on the wrong road—and that General Hood had sent him to show me my position. I inquired when he saw General Hood, and said that, according to the instructions I had received, we were going exactly right. He said he had just come from General Hood. After some further parleying, I concluded (in view of the fact, as General Forrest informed me, that the enemy had abandoned the direct road and taken the Carter's Creek Pike) that General Hood had changed his mind after I left him as to what he wished me to do. So we turned back with this officer to the road we had left and followed it toward Spring Hill (as I supposed)  until we came to the line of troops crossing the road, and here I saw General Brown. I was then informed that I was to march on and form on the right and in extension of Cheatham's troops. This was so directly the reverse of what Hood himself told me he wished—"Put your right across the road beyond Spring Hill, your left extending down this way" (where I saw him soon after crossing the creek); "I do not wish you to march your whole corps up to the right; it is too far for the men"—that I felt sure a mistake had been made. So I said to my staff officers: "Bivouac the men here and I will go to see General Hood and find out what he wishes us to do."

Procuring a guide to Hood's quarters (I think perhaps the staff officer mentioned went with me), I hunted up General Hood. I found him in bed, and asked if he had changed his mind since I saw him last as to what I was to do. He replied that he had not, but that some one had come from Cheatham and represented that his right was exposed. I explained the situation. He replied: "Let the men rest and take the advance to Franklin in the morning."

Now I am wholly unable to say how my troops were located after I left them. When I left, the head of the column was up near where I saw and talked with Brown. I cannot recall the further occurrences of the night, but we were on the road next morning moving toward Franklin — Gen. Alexander P. Stewart

And so at eleven o'clock at night General Hood seemed to have despaired of doing anything with his infantry to check Schofield's retreat to Franklin further than to check stragglers south of Spring Hill, and directed General Stewart to let his men rest and take the advance in the march to Franklin in the morning.

But he had one hope left—a forlorn one, indeed, but still a hope—of being able to check the march north of Spring Hill until daylight, and this was by means of Forrest's Cavalry. Forrest had ridden to Hood's headquarters in company with General Stewart after the latter had bivouacked his column, and seems to have been there in conference with General Hood when General Bate arrived about eleven o'clock.

General Forrest reports that his command was all without ammunition except Jackson's Division, which had captured a supply during the day, and that General Bell had actually made his last forward movement, in concert with Cleburne, with only four rounds per man. But Forrest never pondered over obstacles; and being instructed by General Hood that he had ordered his corps commanders to furnish him a supply and that he must place his cavalry across the pike north of Spring Hill, he left at once to personally see about getting the ammunition, and then moved his command northward.

Finding that the necessary ammunition could not be obtained from Generals Cheatham and Stewart, the cavalry general, nevertheless, ordered Jackson's Division—about 2,000 men—to move northward and seize the pike near Thompson's Station and hold it if possible, and sent a staff officer to guide them to the pike.

Jackson, always prompt, was on the flank of the enemy by 1:30 a.m., and Ross's Brigade made a charge in the darkness, which caused the greatest confusion in the moving wagon train which was on the turnpike at the point reached. Ross's Brigade at this point burned a number of wagons and captured and brought off the teams. General Stanley says of this attack:

> General Cox's Division was out of the way and the train commenced to pull out at one o'clock on the morning of the 30th. The number of wagons, including artillery and ambulances, was about eight hundred. At the very starting point they had to pass singly over a bridge, and it was exceedingly doubtful whether the train could be put in the road by daylight. Unless this could be done and the corps put in motion, we were sure of being attacked at daylight and of being compelled to fight under every disadvantage. I was strongly advised to burn the train and move on with the troops and such wagons as could be saved, but I determined to make an effort to save the train. My staff officers were busily employed hurrying up teamsters, and everything promised well, when we were again thrown into despair by the report that the train was attacked north of Thompson's Station and that the

whole train had been stopped.²⁴

General Kimball's Division was hurried forward, as was also General Wood's Division, which had been deployed just beyond Spring Hill to guard the exit of the wagon train from the town. A small force of Federals from some distance beyond Ross's point of attack had also been moved back, and, meeting the head of the Federal column moving up from the south, the two commands had fired into each other by mistake.

Wayside exhibit discussing the center of the Federal position during the battle, Spring Hill, TN. (Photo Lochlainn Seabrook)

The infantry column was too strong for Jackson. Wood's men, moving off the road to the right, were greatly harassed by the Confederate cavalry; but steadily pressed forward on the flank of the train, which was successfully guarded past the point of danger.

All the trains did not get out of Spring Hill until five o'clock in the morning, and were followed and guarded by Wagner's Division. In the meantime General Schofield, who seems to have thrown off his lethargy, after making up his mind to abandon Columbia, was actively directing the movements of his army. He reached Spring Hill with Ruger's Division at 7 p.m., and at once pushed on with the same command to Thompson's Station to force a passage of the road which he was informed had been seized by the Confederates at that point.

At 10 p.m. Capt. William J. Twining, his aid-de-camp, who had ridden on to Franklin, by instruction of General Schofield, dispatched General Thomas at Nashville:

> Major General Schofield directs me to inform you that the enemy's cavalry crossed Duck River in force at daylight this morning at Huey's Mills, six miles from Columbia, and pushed at once for Spring Hill. Their cavalry reached that point at 4 p.m. and their infantry came in before dark and attacked General Stanley, who held the place with one division, very heavily. General Schofield's troops are pushing for Franklin as rapidly as possible. The General says he will not be able to get farther than Thompson's Station to-night, and possibly not farther than Spring Hill. He regards the situation as extremely perilous, and fears that he may be forced into a general battle to-morrow or lose his wagon train. General Wilson's cavalry have been pushed off toward the east, and do not connect with our infantry nor cover the pike. Thinking that the troops under Gen. A. J. Smith had reached Franklin, General Schofield directed me to have them pushed down the Franklin Pike to Spring Hill to-morrow. I left General Schofield two hours ago at Thompson's Station.

General Schofield's energy and alertness during the late afternoon and night was in marked contrast with the supineness of General Hood. Once aware of the true nature of the crisis with which he was confronted, he pushed forward promptly with Ruger's Division first to the relief of Stanley; and finding things were, owing to the blunders of the Confederate leaders, in fairly good shape at Spring Hill and his enemy asleep in sight of the road, he pushed on in person to Thompson's Station to open the road at that point, which he was informed had been seized by part of Forrest's command.

Returning then to Spring Hill, General Schofield personally superintended the movement forward of the remainder of the army. It is now clearly known that it was he who strongly advised Stanley to "burn the trains and move on with the troops," as stated by that commander. It must be admitted, however, that the handling of the army of Schofield, seconded by the accomplished Stanley, between 6 p.m. of the $29^{th}$ and daylight of the $30^{th}$ was skillful, prompt, and energetic. But had General Hood pursued a like course in the afternoon and taken personal command of his own front, all would have been lost to the Union army.

There are not lacking writers who have striven to demonstrate that General Schofield in the operations of the $29^{th}$ was engaged in a game of profound strategy with General Hood, that he had known Hood at the Military Academy and known him to be a rash blunderer without mathematical capacity or power of combination, and that he (Schofield) had reasoned that Hood would helplessly dally before Spring Hill without power to attack or decide what next should be done.

It is scarcely necessary to point out the weakness of such an argument, which would not be creditable to the intelligence of General Schofield. Indeed, that accomplished and skillful commander made no such claim in his report of the operations; but, on the other hand, from Franklin next day at noon in response to a telegram from General Thomas saying, "If you can prevent Hood from turning your position at Franklin, it should be held; but I do not wish you to risk too much," promptly and frankly replied:

> I am satisfied that I have heretofore run too much risk in trying to hold Hood in check while so far inferior to him in both infantry and cavalry. The slightest mistake on my part or failure of a subordinate during the last few days might have proved disastrous. I do not want to get into so tight a place again, yet I will cheerfully act in accordance with your views of expediency if you think it important to hold Hood back as long as possible.

(Photo Lochlainn Seabrook)

It must be patent to the most casual observer from what has been narrated above that but for the failure of Hood's subordinates to act promptly at Spring Hill Stanley would have been crushed before nightfall, the wagon train and reserve artillery of the army captured, Schofield entrapped as he approached in the darkness with Ruger's Division, and the remaining divisions of Cox, Wood, and Kimball left at the mercy of Hood at daylight next morning.

It was Providence, not strategy, which saved the Union army that night, and a paralysis scarcely less effective than that which overtook the hosts of Sennacherib fell upon the Confederate army as darkness came on, under the shelter of which Schofield's army moved "rapidly and silently" by on their hurried retreat to Franklin.

Success here and the destruction of his antagonist would have placed Hood in a most exalted position among his people and his name high among the great masters of strategy in the war. The move was faultless; the success of it up to 4 p.m. startling. Triumph was within his grasp. But failure came, whatever the cause, where least to be expected among those splendid officers and men. General Schofield has been honored by the nation with the highest military office in the gift of the people. Hood, failing through no fault of his own, unless it was his failure to personally see that his orders were obeyed, is reckoned by the average reader of history as mediocre and inefficient. But beyond question General Stewart was right in this: Hood, being present on the field, should have given his orders in person, if necessary, and personally seen that they were obeyed. The fault was not with Cheatham. There is no evidence that he failed in any respect. But General Hood might have seen that no mistakes were made by any one.[25] — J. P. YOUNG, C.S.A.

## FROM A SOLDIER IN THE 20TH TENNESSEE, C.S.A.

☛ On Nov. 21, 1864, Hood began crossing his army over the Tennessee at Tuscumbia and Florence, heading it towards Columbia, Tenn., on the Waynesboro Road. On the 29th he crossed Duck River three miles above Columbia with Cheatham's and Stewart's corps and one division of Lee's corps, crossing Rutherford Creek some five miles north of Duck River, and marched to Spring Hill.

The Yankee Army in this section was about 23,000 infantry and 5,500 cavalry, total 28,500, under General Schofield (who commanded Sherman's left wing in the Georgia campaign). On the 29th, Hood, after traversing the fields and by-roads with his army, late in the afternoon was in position with his front corps (Cheatham's) within two or three hundred yards east of the Columbia pike at Spring Hill, which was twelve miles in rear of Schofield's position at Columbia. This flank movement of Hood's caused Schofield to retreat in haste back to Spring Hill, and that night on to Franklin.

The main Yankee column did not reach Spring Hill until late in the evening or night, when Cheatham's corps lay within two hundred yards of this retreating column and heard them passing almost the entire night without firing scarcely a gun, when the object of the flank movement was to throw the Confederate forces across the pike at Spring Hill and force Schofield to attack or surrender. Now whose fault was it, on the part of the Confederates, that the attack was not made? This mistake and failure caused a great deal of talk and criticism from the Southern soldiers and historians. From the evidence the fault seems to lie between Generals Hood and Cheatham, and the reports of these two gallant and patriotic soldiers, as well as that of some division commanders of Cheatham's corps, will be submitted in full, and see if we can help to clear the public mind on this unfortunate affair.

General Hood, in his report of this affair, made December 11,1864, said:

> Major-General Cheatham was ordered at once to attack the enemy vigorously and get possession of the pike at Spring Hill (the road to Franklin), and although these orders were frequently and earnestly repeated, he made but a feeble and partial attack, failing to reach the point indicated.

Again, in his [Hood's] history of the campaign, *Advance and Retreat*, it is related:

> General Stewart was then ordered to proceed to the right of Cheatham and

place his corps across the pike north of Spring Hill. By this hour, however, twilight was upon us, when General Cheatham rode up in person. I at once directed Stewart to halt, and turning to Cheatham I exclaimed with deep emotion, as I felt the golden opportunity fast slipping from me, "General, why in the name of God have you not attacked the enemy and taken possession of the pike?"

Lieutenant-General Stewart, referring to this statement in a published letter, says, "No such exclamation by Hood to Cheatham could have been made in my presence."

Major-General Cheatham gave the following account of the affair at Spring Hill:

> In pursuance of orders from army headquarters, my command crossed Duck River on the morning of Nov. 29, 1864, the division of Major-General Cleburne in advance, followed by that of Major-General Bate, the division of Major-General Brown in the rear. The march was made as rapidly as the condition of the road would allow and without occurrence of note, until about 3 p.m., when I arrived at Rutherford's Creek, two and one-half miles from Spring Hill. At this point General Hood gave me verbal orders as follows: That I should get Cleburne across the creek and send him forward toward Spring Hill, with instructions to communicate with General Forrest, who was near the village, ascertain from him the position of the enemy, and attack immediately; that I should remain at the creek, and assist General Bate in crossing his division, and then go forward and put Bate's command in to support Cleburne, and that he should push Brown forward to join me.
> 
> As soon as the division of General Bate had crossed the creek I rode forward, and at a point on the road, about one and a half miles from Spring Hill, I saw the left of Cleburne's command just disappearing over the hill to the left of the road. Halting there, I waited a few minutes for the arrival of Bate, and formed his command with his right upon Cleburne's left, and ordered him forward to the support of Cleburne. Shortly after Bate's division had disappeared over the same range of hills, I heard firing towards Cleburne's right, and just then General Brown's division came up. I thereupon ordered Brown to proceed to the right, turn the range of hills over which Cleburne and Bate had crossed, and form line of battle and attack to the right of Cleburne. The division of General Brown was in motion to execute this order when I received a message from Cleburne that his right brigade had been struck in flank by the enemy and had suffered severely, and that he had been compelled to fall back and reform his division with a change of front.
> 
> It so happened that the direction of Cleburne's advance was such as had exposed his right flank to the enemy's line. When his command was formed on the road by which he had marched from Rutherford's Creek, neither the village of Spring Hill nor the turnpike could be seen. Instead of advancing

(Photo Lochlainn Seabrook)

directly upon Spring Hill, his forward movement was a little south of west and almost parallel with the turnpike toward Columbia, instead of northwest upon the enemy's lines, south and east of the village. A reference to the map [at the front of this book] will show Cleburne's line of advance. General Cleburne was killed in the assault upon Franklin the next day, and I had no opportunity to learn from him how it was that the error of direction occurred.

Meanwhile General Bate, whom I had placed in position on the left of Cleburne's line of march, continued to move forward in the same direction until he had reached the farm of N. F. Cheairs [Rippavilla], one and a half miles south of Spring Hill.

After Brown had reached the position indicated to him and had formed a line of battle, he sent to inform me that it would be certain disaster for him to attack, as the enemy's line extended beyond his right several hundred yards. I sent word to him to throw back his right brigade and make the attack. I had already sent couriers after General Bate to bring him back and direct him to join Cleburne's left. Going to the right of my line I found Generals Brown and Cleburne, and the latter reported that he had reformed his division. I then gave orders to Brown and Cleburne that as soon as they could connect their lines they should attack the enemy, who were then in sight; informing them at the same time that General Hood had just told me that Stewart's column was close at hand, and that General Stewart had been ordered to go to my right and place his command across the pike. I furthermore said to them that I would go myself and see that Bate was placed in position to connect with them, and immediately rode to the left of my line for that purpose.

During all this time I had met and talked with General Hood repeatedly, our field headquarters being not over one hundred yards apart. After Cleburne's repulse I had been along my line and had seen that Brown's right was outflanked several hundred yards. I had urged General Hood to hurry up Stewart and place him on my right, and had received from him assurance that this would be done; and this assurance, as before stated, I had communicated to Generals Brown and Cleburne.

When I returned from my left, where I had been to get Bate in position, and was on my way to the right of my line, it was dark; but I intended to move forward with Cleburne and Brown and make the attack, knowing that Bate would be in position to support them. Stewart's column had already passed by on the way toward the turnpike, and I presumed that he would be in position on my right.

On reaching the road where General Hood's field quarters had been established, I found a courier with a message from General Hood requesting me to come to him at Captain Thompson's house [Oaklawn], about one and a fourth miles back on the road to Rutherford's Creek. Here I found Generals Stewart and Hood. The Commanding General there informed me that he had concluded to wait till morning, and directed me to hold my command in readiness to attack at daylight.

I was never more astonished than when General Hood informed me that he had concluded to postpone the attack until daylight. The road was still open—orders to remain quiet until morning—and nothing to prevent the enemy from marching to Franklin.

The following communication, written by Governor (afterward Senator) Harris of Tennessee, then acting as aide to General Hood, is a valuable contribution to the history of this campaign. It is copied from Drake's *Annals of the Army of Tennessee* [C.S.A.] for May, 1877. A copy was furnished to General Hood.

Gov. James D. Porter:—Dear Sir: In answer to yours of the 12$^{th}$ inst., I have to say that on the night that the army of Tennessee, under command of Gen. J. B. Hood, halted at Spring Hill on its march from Columbia to Nashville, General Hood, his adjutant-general Major Mason, and myself occupied the same room at the residence of Captain Thompson, near the village. Late at night we were aroused by a private soldier, who reported to General Hood that on reaching the camp near Spring Hill, he found himself within the Federal lines; that the troops were in great confusion, a part of them were marching in the direction of Franklin, others had turned towards Columbia, and that the road was blocked with baggage-wagons and gun-carriages, rendering it impossible to move in either direction.

(Photo Lochlainn Seabrook)

Upon the receipt of this report, General Hood directed Major Mason to order General Cheatham to move down on the road immediately and attack the enemy. General Hood and myself remained in bed. I went to sleep, and I supposed that General Hood did the same. At daylight on the following morning we learned that the Federal army had left Spring Hill and was being concentrated at Franklin.

On the march to Franklin, General Hood spoke to me, in the presence of Major Mason, of the failure of General Cheatham to make the night attack at Spring Hill, and censured him in severe terms for his disobedience of orders. Soon after this, being alone with Major Mason, the latter remarked that "General Cheatham was not to blame about the matter last night. I did not send him the order." I asked if he had communicated the fact to General Hood. He answered that he had not. I replied that it is due to General Cheatham that this explanation should be made. Thereupon Major Mason joined General Hood and gave him the information.

Afterwards General Hood said to me that he had done injustice to General Cheatham, and requested me to inform him that he held him blameless for the failure at Spring Hill. And, on the day following the battle of Franklin, I was informed by General Hood that he had addressed a note to General Cheatham, assuring him that he did not censure or charge him with the failure to make the attack. Very respectfully, Isham G. Harris. Memphis, Tenn., May 20, 1877.

Maj.-Gen. John C. Brown, commanding Cheatham's division, gave the following account of the same affair:

> My division comprised four brigades of infantry, commanded respectively by Gen. S. R. Gist, of South Carolina, Generals O. F. Strahl, G. W. Gordon, and John C. Carter, of Tennessee. On the morning of Nov. 29, 1864, when I left my bivouac on the Mooresville turnpike in front of Columbia, Tenn., the whole command numbered not exceeding 2,750 effective men. Gist's brigade was the largest, and Strahl's was next in numerical strength; those of Gordon and Carter being about equal in the number of effective men.
> 
> We started on the march about sunrise, and after traversing cedar brakes and pathless woods, crossed Duck River by a pontoon previously laid, about four miles above Columbia, at or near what was known as Davis' Ferry or Davis' Ford. Conforming to the daily alterations, my division was the rear of your [Cheatham's] corps.
> 
> After crossing Duck River, as I now recollect, at or near Bear Creek, the commanding general, apprehending an attack on our left flank, ordered your corps, on its march from that point, to move in two parallel columns, so that it could come instantly into action in two lines of battle if attacked on the flank. Accordingly, my division was ordered to form the supporting column, and for that purpose to leave the road by which the main body was moving, and so conform its movements to that of the other two divisions (Cleburne's and Bate's), that in coming into action to meet an attack on our left flank, it would occupy a place in rear of and about four hundred yards distant from the front line of battle.
> 
> The march thence to Rutherford's Creek was made pursuant to these orders, and the whole distance thus traversed (five or six miles) was through fields and woods and over rough ground, adding greatly to the fatigues of the day. About the commencement of this movement, or soon afterwards, by the order of the commanding general in person, the whole of Gist's and about one-half of Strahl's brigade were detached for picket duty, to be relieved by the orders of the commanding general, thus leaving me with about one-half of my division.
> 
> When near Rutherford's Creek, learning that a crossing was not practicable east of the road, I changed the direction of the march to the left into the road, and found Bate's division preparing to cross the stream. After reaching the north bank of the stream, I was ordered to pursue the road leading in the direction of the Caldwell place [Forrest's headquarters], while Cleburne's and Bate's divisions moved at an angle to the left; but before reaching the Dr. Caldwell house, I was ordered to change the direction of my column to the left, and we reached the "Lewisburg," or "Rally Hill" pike, near the toll-gate, a distance of one and a half miles from Spring Hill.
> 
> This was within an hour or an hour and a half of sunset. I could distinctly see the enemy in force, both infantry and artillery, at Spring Hill, but did not, and perhaps could not at that point, see either troops or wagons moving on the Columbia pike. Forrest's cavalry were on higher ground northeast of my position.
> 
> I was ordered to form a line of battle and "take" Spring Hill. Gist's brigade and the detachment from Strahl had not reported. I formed my line as speedily as worn out troops could be moved, and after throwing forward

a skirmish line, advanced four hundred or five hundred yards, when I discovered a line of the enemy thrown out of Spring Hill, across and threatening my right flank, and I then discovered for the first time that General Forrest's cavalry, which I had been assured would protect my right, had been ordered to another part of the field, leaving me without any protection on my right flank or support in rear. I had neither artillery nor cavalry, and was left in a position where I must meet with inevitable disaster, if I advanced on Spring Hill.

The Caldwell House, Forrest's headquarters during the Battle of Spring Hill. (Photo Lochlainn Seabrook)

    A hasty consultation with my brigade commanders resulted in a determination to suspend the advance, and confer with the corps commander. I need not remind you that in a very few minutes you were upon the field, and fully approved of what had been done, as did also General Hood a little later, when he directed that the attack be delayed until the arrival of Generals Stewart and Gist, and in the meanwhile, that the whole command should be held under orders to advance at a moment's notice. General Gist's brigade reported a little after nightfall, and was immediately placed in position on my right. General Stewart's corps came up later, and went into bivouac on the stream in the rear of my right, where it remained until the following morning. I received no further orders that evening or during the night to advance or change my position. After daylight on the morning of the 30th I took up the line of march for Franklin, the enemy in the meantime having preceded, under circumstances of which you are fully advised.

    On the march to Franklin, General Cleburne, with whom I had long enjoyed very close personal relations, sent a message to the head of my column requesting an interview. Allowing my column to pass on, I awaited his arrival. When he came up, we rode apart from the column through the fields, and he told me with much feeling that he had heard that the commanding general was endeavoring to place upon him the responsibility for allowing the enemy to pass our position on the night previous. I replied to him that I had heard nothing on that subject, and that I hoped he was mistaken. He said, "No, I think not; my information comes through a very reliable channel." He said that he could not afford to rest under such an imputation, and should certainly have the matter investigated to the fullest extent, as soon as we were away from the immediate presence of the enemy.

General Cleburne was quite angry, and evidently was deeply hurt, believing that the commander-in-chief had censured him. I asked General Cleburne who was responsible for the escape of the enemy during the afternoon and night previous. In reply to that inquiry he indulged in some criticisms of a command occupying a position on his left, and concluded by saying that of course the responsibility rested with the commander-in-chief, as he was upon the field during the afternoon, and was fully advised during the night of the movement of the enemy.

The conversation at this point was abruptly terminated by the arrival of orders for yourself from the commanding general. As he left he said. "We will resume this conversation at the first convenient moment," but in less than three hours after that time this gallant soldier was a corpse upon the bloody field of Franklin. — Maj.-Gen. John C. Brown

Major-General Bate, referring to an interview with General Hood between the hours of 10 and 12 of the night of the 29th of November, at which General Bate mentioned a conflict in the orders of the general commanding, and the corps commanders touching the movement of his division, relates that General Hood said:

> It makes no difference now, or it is all right, anyhow, for General Forrest, as you see, has just left, and informed me that he holds the turnpike with a portion of his forces north of Spring Hill, and will stop the enemy if he tries to pass toward Franklin, and so in the morning we will have a surrender without a fight.

He further said in a congratulatory manner, "We can sleep quietly to-night."

General Forrest reported that after the arrival of Cleburne's division at Spring Hill:

> I ordered Brig.-Gen. W. H. Jackson to move with his division in the direction of Thompson's Station and there intercept the enemy. He struck the road at Fitzgerald's, four miles from Spring Hill, at 11 p.m., just as the front of the enemy's column had passed. This attack was a complete surprise, producing much panic and confusion. Brigadier General Jackson had possession of the pike, and fought the enemy until daylight, but receiving no support he was compelled to retire.

Two small brigades, commanded by Brigadier-Generals Armstrong and Ross, constituted Jackson's division. If an adequate force had been sent forward to take advantage of the panic and confusion created by Jackson's attack, a second golden opportunity would not have been lost.

The first intimation of dissatisfaction on the part of the commanding general at the management of the affair at Spring Hill was suggested by the receipt of the following note, written in front of Nashville and dated December 3, 1864:

> My Dear General [Cheatham]: I do not censure you for the failure at Spring Hill. I am satisfied that you are not responsible for it. I witnessed the splendid manner in which you delivered battle at Franklin on the 30th ult., and I now have a higher estimate of you as a soldier than I ever had. Yours very truly, J. B. Hood, General.

"On the morning of the 4th of December," says General Cheatham,

> I went to the headquarters of General Hood, and referring to his note and criticism that had evidently been made by some one, I said to him, "A great opportunity was lost at Spring Hill, but you know that I obeyed your orders there, as everywhere, literally and promptly." General Hood not only did not dissent from what I said, but exhibited the most cordial manner, coupled with confidence and friendship.

William J. McMurray.

After the failure of the Confederates on the night of November 29 to cut off the Yankee army at Spring Hill, Hood put his army in motion the next morning and arrived in front of Franklin, 11 miles north of Spring Hill, about 2 p.m. Here he found General Schofield with the fourth and twenty-third army corps under General Stanley and Cox respectively, numbering 23,734 infantry and artillery, and 5,500 cavalry, entrenched behind two lines of earthworks.[26] — DR. WILLIAM JOSIAH MCMURRAY, C.S.A.

## AN UNUSUAL NIGHT AT SPRING HILL

☞ A memorable night, to many Tennesseans especially, was that at Palmetto, Ga., after the eventful campaign at Rocky Face, near Dalton, to Atlanta and back to Jonesboro and then to Lovejoy Station. The Federal troops had fallen back to Atlanta, and the Confederate army had moved across to the village of Palmetto, on the Atlanta and West Point road. This was September 19, 1864.

A truce of ten days having occurred for exchange of prisoners, there was absolute cessation of hostilities, a welcome diversion from nearly three months of excessive fighting. President Davis, Howell Cobb (of

Georgia), and Gov. Harris (of Tennessee) were speakers on the night mentioned, and the Tennessee campaign was the theme. The wind blew briskly, tattered battle flags were grouped about the place for speaking, flapping over the pine fires, and when the President said we were to go into Tennessee there was indeed wild enthusiasm among those who were ready to face any foes and undergo all possible privations to breathe the air and greet the loved ones in their native State. Soldiers from all the States pulsated with wild enthusiasm.

Rattle and Snap, Mt. Pleasant, TN. (Photo Lochlainn Seabrook)

The march across the country was full of interest. Sometimes rations were acorns and crab apples, but the men were buoyant with the prospects ahead. On reaching the rich lands of Maury County, near Mt. Pleasant, and marching across to Columbia by the magnificent estates of Polk [Rattle and Snap], Pillow [Clifton Place], Granbury, and others, such joy filled the hearts of Tennesseans as they had never realized before.

Sunday the army rested about Columbia, and Monday morning, November 29, a large part of it crossed Duck River a few miles above the town on a pontoon bridge that was ready at early dawn. The marching was in the direction of Spring Hill, and the confidence in Gen. Hood was such that he would surely cut off the escape of all the Federals who had not already passed on the Nashville pike.

The head of the column arrived at Spring Hill about an hour before sunset, and commands were deployed promptly, ready for any command. Delay of movement there became inexplicable. We were in plain view of the Federals, who had tumbled fences for hasty breastworks. Officers dashed back and forth along the lines, evidently expecting a mad rush of Confederates. We waited until darkness, but even into the night we fully expected orders to break their lines and secure the pike. By and by fires were built by the thousands, it seemed, and we remained as tranquil through the night as if the war were over, and poor, silly fellows we were to believe that the day of our redemption was at hand.

Morning came, and we moved out the pike toward Nashville. As evidence of the condition of the enemy, the writer counted thirty-four wagons that had been abandoned on the way, and in some instances all four of the mules to a wagon had been killed to prevent their capture.[27] — SUMNER ARCHIBALD CUNNINGHAM, C.S.A.

## GENERALS JOHN BELL HOOD & STEPHEN DILL LEE

☛ It is well known that Gen. Hood entertained the highest regard for Gen. Lee's ability. [In] his book, *Advance and Retreat*, he uses this language: "I might assert with equal assurance that, had Lieut. Gen. Lee been in advance at Spring Hill the previous afternoon, Schofield's army would never have passed that point." I merely mention this extract to show his exalted opinion of Gen. Lee.[28] — LOUIS F. GARRARD, CONFEDERATE CORRESPONDENT

## MEMORIES OF THE CONFLICT AT SPRING HILL

☛ . . . By a flank movement General Hood succeeded in placing several divisions of his army on the east of Spring Hill, thus eluding the bulk of the Federal army, which lay at Columbia. . . . At Spring Hill we saw but one position which could possibly be utilized, and it seemed certain death to try to reach that. There were a few large oak trees left standing on the north side of the road and in less than five hundred yards of the Federal works. If we could only get there, we could whip all the artillery they could bring to bear on the division.

Confederate Lieutenant [John M.] Ozanne ordered us forward in single file, with instructions to reach the trees if possible. Then commenced a race for life. It seemed certain that they would see our object and kill us all before we reached the trees. But we knew the importance of the position and made up our minds to gain it or lose our lives, and all ran as fast as they could. The tree nearest the road was the largest one, and I outran all the rest and got safely to it. The others filed to the right, and each got safely behind a tree. It was a hard run of over half a mile, and before we got calmed down we saw the wicked looking mouths of a battery of Napoleon guns pointing at the lane near the river.

I think we fired at four hundred and fifty yards' elevation, and the way we did that battery up was simply wonderful. In less than twenty minutes, and before their gunners had got the right elevation, we had driven them from their position. Soon Brown's Division had formed at right angles to the road on the north, its left resting on the road. This battery or another took position in the northeast edge of the town and attempted to shell the division in the field, the distance being about twelve hundred yards. Then again our guns played upon them with such savage effect that after a desperate struggle they were driven from the field and did not show themselves again. The division remained in line of battle in the field unmolested till dark, and we had to remain behind our trees until the darkness would hide our withdrawal.

Some years ago somebody intimated that General Cheatham's Division, commanded by General Brown, ought to have advanced promptly against the Federals. The truth is, it ought to have done no such thing. The Federal line of infantry, about three-quarters of a mile long, ran northeast from the town [of Spring Hill]. Cheatham's line ran about north and south, and was about half as long as the Federal line. If Cheatham had advanced, the Federals would have swung around in his rear.

After we had whipped the Federal batteries off the field and I was leisurely loading my gun, I saw a large man standing on the works and facing east. I called the attention of the men to him and asked them to watch him, as I intended to punish him for his impudence. A trifling circumstance occurred just as I got the bullet down, and I let go the ramrod to adjust my clothing, which was ragged and had caught on the hammer of my gun. Being in a hurry, I forgot to withdraw the ramrod, and, hastily capping my gun, I called out to the men to watch my man.

I fired at him, and the recoil of that gun was simply terrific; it knocked me down and away back from the tree. I fell full length, and hardly had sense enough to get back to the tree. My gun punched me in the ribs, nearly dislocated my shoulder, skinned my jaw and the side of my head, knocked my hat off, and sprang out of my hands.

After a few minutes I got my breath freely and found that I was not killed, and I called out: "Boys, what became of the Yankee?" The reply was: "Both fell backward at the report of the gun." Now if that Yankee is living and is drawing a pension, he ought to divide with me, for if I had not shot the ramrod at him he would not have lived to make the application, and in shooting the ramrod I was worse hurt than he was. If we had not gained the position behind the trees, that battery would have cut the division to pieces or driven it back under the bank of the creek for protection.

Part of Spring Hill's original town commons on the northwest section of the village, where the Union army parked some 800 "wheeled vehicles" on November 29, 1864. This portion of the "park" is now farmland, and housing developments are quickly encroaching. (Photo Lochlainn Seabrook)

This incident illustrates two points in our peculiar service: First, that much was expected of us by the rank and file of our division, and, secondly, the desperate chances we took and the alacrity with which we fought their artillery. We never failed to silence or drive from the field a Federal battery under favorable circumstances.

The next morning after our sharp practice at Spring Hill we reported early to division headquarters, and with cleaned guns and replenished cartridge boxes took our position in front of the division and began the march to Franklin. Our division being the front one, we were the foremost infantry in our army. The Federal army had passed Spring Hill during the night, and we were following them. Nothing occurred of note until we arrived within a few miles of Franklin, when a battery was observed on a hill near the road.[29] — ISAAC N. STANNON, C.S.A.

"THE SAD MISTAKE"
☛ A few of us "old boys" yet remain who remember how severe were the times when Hood's army marched from Lovejoy Station, in Georgia, to Nashville, Tenn. . . . [From Florence, Alabama we] marched for Tennessee. The weather was very bad. We encountered rain, snow, ice, and mud. Orders were very strict. We were forbidden to straggle, forage, kill any hogs, or visit any hen houses, yet some such things were done. Two boys who killed a hog which they said "tried" to "bite" them were overtaken by one of our generals, who made them carry the hog suspended from a fence rail all day.

It was snowing hard one evening late when we stopped to camp for the night, and some of the boys cut down a tree, which fell on others, killing three of them. Another night in desperation some of the boys went to "Marse Frank's" headquarters and took a barrel of "hard-tack" from his tent, and also a nicely cooked ham of fresh pork. One day we heard cheering in front of us; and when we got to the State line, we found suspended from one tree to another across the road a canvas with the inscription: "Tennessee, a Grave or a Free Home." Then we knew what the cheering meant.

Proudly we marched across the State line under the canvas, thinking whether it would be a grave or a free home. We marched the quickstep to Columbia. Then Cheatham's Corps flanked Columbia and crossed Duck River some four miles above, and made a forced march to cut off Schofield's army at Spring Hill. What a tiresome march that was! We reached Spring Hill about sunset. We all remember the sad mistake made there when, on the 29th of November, 1864, we slept on arms within gunshot of our enemies, who were passing up the turnpike for Franklin in the most confused manner—infantry, cavalry, artillery, wagons, and ambulances in a conglomeration. It was some one's fault that Schofield's army was not captured or cut off that night, and that awful slaughter at Franklin would have been averted.

Some of us went into the Yankee lines that night, and on reporting to our general heard the conditions discussed.

On the morning of the 30th we started for Franklin. By the roadside we saw many wagons with the teams killed in harness, giving evidence of the presence of our cavalry and the consternation of the enemy.[30] — H. K. NELSON, C.S.A.

## EXPERIENCES ON THE HOOD CAMPAIGN

☞ [Regarding the essay by Union officer J. P. Young, "Hood's Failure at Spring Hill," located in the "Union Recollections" of this book:] I was a private in the 1st Missouri Artillery, with General Polk's command, which formed a junction with [Joseph E.] Johnston's army at Adairsville, Ga., May 17, 1864. Just one year from that day I, with others, took refuge behind the intrenchments of Vicksburg, Miss. I was with that army all through the Georgia and Tennessee campaigns, and surrendered under Johnston at Greensboro, N.C.

John B. Hood.

When Johnston was superseded by Hood, the soldiers were very much depressed at losing their noble commander, in whom they had implicit confidence. This was one of the most crushing blows the Army of Tennessee ever suffered. Hood's movements from then on were a series of failures.

I was very much surprised when I read the account by Judge Young. Although I was with Stewart's Corps, I was unaware of such maneuvering north of Duck River. If his description is correct, Hood certainly did make a great failure.

On November 29 our battery received orders to select the best horses of the company and report to General Stewart with four guns, one ordnance wagon, and no caissons—we were the only artillery company with the corps. We joined the infantry and crossed Duck River four miles east of Columbia at Davis's Ferry on a pontoon and reported to Brigadier General Brant to bring up the rear. We were requested to make as little noise as possible, for fear of detection by the enemy. During our circuitous march we were interrupted by the whistle of Minies several times. The road (if any) over which we passed was very rough and rocky, and when night came it was very dark. We had to feel our way through the timber; and when crossing one of the huge boulders every spoke in one of the rear wheels on the gun to which I belonged was smashed, and to our surprise the extra wheel on the ordnance wagon would not fit. We appropriated the hind wheel of a near-by farmer's wagon and moved on. After a circuitous march of what seemed about twenty miles, we stopped at midnight for a short rest. Owing to having to replace our broken wheel and short rest, the infantry were considerably in our advance, and we were ordered to push forward as rapidly as possible and overtake them, in which we succeeded just as day was breaking on the morning of the 30$^{th}$ a short distance from the Nashville Pike, to find that the Federals had passed on in the direction of Franklin.

Next came the battle of Franklin, about which I will only say it was the hardest-fought battle in which I was ever engaged. I always thought Hood could have avoided so much bloodshed by flanking and accomplished as much or more good.[31] — SAM B. DUNLAP, C.S.A.

## THE SPRING HILL DEFEAT & FRANKLIN
☛ . . . Hood was delayed at Tuscumbia and Florence for twenty days before he could get the necessary clothing, ammunition, and provisions to enable him to march into Tennessee. He had arranged for these supplies to meet him on arrival at Tuscumbia, and he was much embarrassed at the delay, which of course lessened the chances of success for him, as it enabled the enemy to prepare and concentrate to meet him. He finally got off about November 20. The enemy fell back from Pulaski and other points as soon as he started toward Columbia and Nashville. Hood's advance was at Columbia on November 26. Two corps of the enemy were at this point. On the night of the 27th the enemy evacuated Columbia, taking a strong position on the opposite side of the Duck River, prepared to dispute it's passage. Their advance was in strong rifle pits two hundred and fifty yards from the river bank.

General Hood determined by a rapid march to try to reach the rear of the enemy near Spring Hill. He took Cheatham's and Stewart's Corps and Johnston's Division of Lee's Corps and commenced the movement on the night of the 28th and 29th of November. Lee, with his two remaining divisions, was directed to occupy and hold the enemy in his position opposite Columbia till Hood could reach Spring Hill on the 29th. Lee early on the 29th commenced demonstrating to cross by the use and display of pontoons with artillery demonstration. He held the enemy until past midday, and in the evening crossed some of his troops and captured the rifle pits of the enemy in a most gallant charge made by his Alabama brigade of Stevenson's Division, under command of Brig. Gen. E. W. Pettus. The troops of the enemy were held (most of them) till long after dark on the 29th. The last of them left Lee's front about 2 a.m. on the 30th of November, Lee pursuing and reaching Spring Hill by 9 a.m. on the 30th of November, while Hood with his two corps reached Spring Hill the afternoon of the 29th long before dark, and why the enemy was not fought and captured at Spring Hill is yet a mystery.

Before starting from Columbia it was understood that the first troops reaching the pike at Spring Hill should cross it or commence fighting and would be supported and reenforced by the other troops as they arrived in succession on the field. A lodgment was to be made on the pike and the march of the enemy stopped. Lee was to follow the enemy as they moved from Columbia and attack in their rear. Forrest's Cavalry and Cheatham's Corps were in advance. Only a small division of the enemy was encountered. No serious engagement took place. Stewart's Corps arrived before dark. The enemy almost in a panic passed all night along the pike at a double-quick—wagons, artillery, etc. Our troops were in bivouac not eight hundred yards from the pike, seeing and hearing it all, and no serious attempt was made to stop it. A simple advance of one division a few hundred yards would have secured the pike. A few rounds of artillery would have routed the enemy.

Stragglers from the enemy came into our camps to light their pipes and were captured, believing we were their friends. The movement was well executed by Hood's two corps. The conception of the whole plan was brilliant and well executed, all but the fighting at the critical moment. Lee did his part, and after a march of twelve or fifteen miles was on hand at Spring Hill at 9 a.m. on the morning of the 30$^{th}$ to take a hand. Rumor said it was the fault of the commander of the leading corps. His friends said Hood was near enough to have enforced his orders and to have seen that they were executed.

Historical marker, Columbia, TN. (Photo Lochlainn Seabrook)

Some one at this late date should be made responsible for the egregious blunder, mistake, or disobedience, as it certainly entailed the next day a terrible slaughter on as gallant an army as ever went into battle at Franklin. The slaughter, too, was inflicted by the same troops that were at the mercy of the Confederates the previous evening and night. The enemy having escaped at Spring Hill without a fight, Hood put his troops on march to follow them up toward Franklin, Stewart's Corps in advance, then Cheatham's, then Lee's. Hood found the enemy intrenched at Franklin, and he determined to fight and carry the place and, if possible, whip them before reaching Nashville. Lee's Corps (two divisions), having advanced from Columbia by a forced march, moved leisurely forward from Spring Hill [to Franklin. By the end of the next day] . . . six [Confederate] general officers and about five thousand men had fallen; whole aggregations were almost destroyed. Most of the broken troops, however, stuck to the works, and across the narrow embankment a terrible hand-to-hand conflict was carried on with rifle and bayonet far into the night. . . .[32] — STEPHEN DILL LEE, C.S.A.

## GEN. ALEXANDER P. STEWART'S VIEW OF SPRING HILL

☛ My attention has been called to some statements made in a book published in 1907 by Charles Scribner's Sons, New York, entitled *Military Memoirs of a Confederate: A Critical Narrative*, by E. [Edward] P. [Porter]

Alexander, brigadier general in the Confederate army, chief of artillery Longstreet's Corps.

These statements . . . constitute very serious charges against Gen. B. F. Cheatham and myself, which, if true, should have subjected us both to the severest penalties. So far as I am individually concerned, they are absolutely false and without foundation. I do not believe they are true so far as General Cheatham is concerned.

Describing the events of the Confederate war that took place in the fall of 1864, the campaign made by Gen. John B. Hood, in command of the Army of Tennessee, into Tennessee and his lamentable failure to attack the enemy near Spring Hill, Tenn., during the afternoon and night of November 29, 1864, the writer [E. P. Alexander] says:

> The issue at stake was now lost by the noncompliance with orders of General Cheatham, commanding one of Hood's Corps.
> 
> Schofield had taken position on the north side of Duck River, opposing Hood's crossing. Hood left Lee's Corps to demonstrate against Schofield, while he threw a pontoon bridge across the river three miles above, and crossed Cheatham's and Stewart's Corps, which marched to Spring Hill on the Franklin Pike, twelve miles in Schofield's rear, arriving about 3 p.m. This place was held by the second division of the 4$^{th}$ Corps, about four thousand strong. Hood's force was about eighteen thousand infantry. Hood took Cheatham with Cleburne, a division commander, within sight of the pike, along which the enemy could now be seen retreating at double-quick with wagons in a trot, and gave explicit orders for an immediate attack and occupation of the pike. Similar orders, too, were given to Stewart's Corps; and when Hood found later that nothing was being done, he sent more messages by staff officers, which also failed of effect. The head of Schofield's infantry arrived about nine o'clock, and passed unmolested except by some random picket shots to which they made no reply.
> 
> . . . A few days after Cheatham frankly admitted his delinquency. It was rumored that both he and General Stewart had that evening absented themselves from their divisions. Both had been often distinguished for gallantry, and Hood now overlooked it, believing it had been a lesson not to be forgotten. Nevertheless it proved the death blow to Hood's army.

In [my] reply to this remarkable tissue of false statements I quote from . . . the *Official Records of the Union and Confederate Armies*:

> To General S. Cooper, Adjutant and Inspector General, Richmond, Va. From Headquarters Army of Tennessee, Near Smithfield Depot, N.C., April 3, 1865.
> 
> Sir: In my report of the operations of my corps during my campaign made by General Hood into Tennessee I omitted the details of what transpired near Spring Hill during the afternoon and night of the 29$^{th}$ of November, 1864. I respectfully submit the following statement and ask that it be filed as a part of my report.

On the morning of November 29 General Hood moved with Cheatham's Corps and mine and Johnson's Division of Lee's Corps (the latter reporting to me), Cheatham's Corps in advance. We made a forced march to get in the rear of the enemy. In the course of the afternoon, about three or four o'clock, I reached Rutherford's Creek as Cheatham's rear division was crossing. I received orders to halt and form on the south side of the creek, my right to rest on or near the creek, so as to move down the creek if necessary. Subsequently I received an order to send a division across the creek, and finally between sunset and dark an order was received to cross the creek, leaving a division on the south side.

Edward Johnson's Division, being in the rear, was designated to remain. Riding in advance of the column about dark, I found General Hood some half a mile from the creek and about as far west of the road on which we were marching and which led to Spring Hill.

The commanding general gave me a young man of the neighborhood as a guide and told me to move on and place my right across the pike beyond Spring Hill, "your left," he added, "extending down this way." This would have placed my line in the rear of Cheatham's, except that my right would have extended beyond his. The guide informed me that at a certain point the road made a sudden turn to the left, going into Spring Hill; that from this bend there used to be a road leading across to the pike, meeting it at the tollgate some mile and a half beyond Spring Hill toward Franklin. I told him if he could find it that was the right road.

Arriving at the bend of the road, we passed through a large gateway, taking what appeared in the darkness to be an indistinct path. Within a short distance I found General Forrest's headquarters [Caldwell House], and stopped to ascertain the position of his pickets covering Cheatham's right and of the enemy. He informed me that his scouts reported the enemy leaving the direct pike—leading from Spring Hill to Franklin and Nashville—and taking the one down Carter's Creek. While in conversation with him I was informed that a staff officer from General Hood had come up and halted the column. It turned out to be a staff (engineer) officer of General Cheatham's, who informed me that General Hood had sent him to place me in position.

It striking me as strange that the commanding general should send an officer not of his own staff on this errand, or indeed any one, as he had given directions to me in person, I inquired of the officer if he had seen General Hood since I had. He replied that he had just come from General Hood, and that the reason why he was sent to me was that I was to go into position on General Brown's right (the right of Cheatham's Corps), and he and General Brown had been over the ground by daylight. Thinking it possible the commanding general had changed his mind as to what he wished me to do, I concluded it was proper to be governed by the directions of this staff officer, and therefore returned to the road and moved on toward Spring Hill. Arriving near the line of Brown's Division, General Brown explained his

Alexander P. Stewart.

position, which was oblique to the pike, his right being farther from it than his left.

It was evident that if my command were marched up and formed on his right (it being now a late hour) it would require all night to accomplish it, and the line, instead of extending across the pike, would bear away from it. Feeling satisfied there was a mistake, I directed the troops to be bivouacked while I rode back to find the commanding general to explain my situation and get further instructions. On arriving at his quarters I inquired of him if he had sent this officer of General Cheatham's staff to place me in position. He replied that he had. I next inquired if he had changed his mind as to what he wished me to do. He replied that he had not, "But," said he, "the fact is, General Cheatham has been here and represented that somebody ought to be somebody on Brown's right." I explained to him that in the uncertainty I was in I had directed the troops, who had been marching rapidly since daylight (and it was now it 11 p.m.), to be placed in bivouac, and had come to report. He remarked in substance that it was not material; to let the men rest; and directed me to move before daylight in the morning, taking the advance toward Franklin.

Subsequently General Hood made to me this statement: "I wish you and your people to understand that I attach no blame to you for the failure at Spring Hill. On the contrary, I know if I had had you there the attack would have been made."

Very respectfully, General, your obedient servant, Alex P. Stewart, Lieutenant General.

Later Letter from General Hood—Chester, S.C., April 9, 1865.

My Dear General [Stewart]: Before leaving for Texas I desire to say that I am sorry to know that some of your friends thought that I intended some slight reflection on your conduct at Spring Hill. You did all that I could say or claim that I would have done under similar circumstances. The great opportunity passed with daylight. Since I have been informed that your friends felt that my report led to uncertainty as to yourself and troops. I regret that I did not make myself more clear in my report by giving more in detail about the staff officer of General Cheatham's. I only regret, General, that I did not have you with your corps in front on that day. I feel, and have felt, that Tennessee to-day would have been in our possession. . . Your friend, J. B. Hood.

Volume XLV, Part I, serial 93 of the *Official Records of the Union and Confederate Armies* was published in 1894; this "Critical Narrative" was published in 1907. It would seem that if the author of the latter had wished to be accurate and just he would have consulted the "Official Records."

Speaking of the battle of Franklin, he [Gen. E. P. Alexander] says: "To assault was a terrible proposition to troops who during Johnston's long retreat had been trained to avoid charging breastworks." What breastworks were in their way which it was necessary to charge? This writer has evidently accepted as true General Hood's claim that the Army of Tennessee was demoralized by General Johnston's conduct of the Atlanta campaign. There could not be a greater mistake. If anything could have demoralized that army, it would have been the removal of General Johnston from the command of it and the substitution of General Hood.

The truth is, the failure at Spring Hill was General Hood's own failure. He was at the front with the advanced troops, or could have been, and should have been; and if he gave "explicit orders for an immediate attack and occupation of the pike" and they were disobeyed, the remedy was entirely in his own hands. If it had been true that Cheatham and I disobeyed orders to make an immediate attack and absented ourselves from our commands that evening and Hood had overlooked such offenses, that would have demonstrated his incapacity for the chief command.

The author of the "Critical Narrative" excuses the attack on Franklin on the ground that Hood saw no alternative, since he had lost the one opportunity of the campaign at Spring Hill the night before. The loss at Spring Hill could have been fully retrieved at Franklin by crossing the Harpeth River by the fords above Franklin and getting a strong position among the Brentwood hills in the rear of the enemy.

Of what value is a "Critical Narrative" made up from "rumor?" It is worse than a waste of time to read such a book.[33] — ALEXANDER P. STEWART, C.S.A.

## FURTHER CLARIFICATIONS FROM GEN. A. P. STEWART

☞ Hood had maneuvered skillfully and had completely entrapped Schofield, and then allowed him to escape. Schofield at Columbia was confronted by S. D. Lee's Corps, who menaced his front; while Forrest was sent to the right, and, crossing Duck River, drove back Wilson's Cavalry to a point beyond Spring Hill, leaving Schofield's left uncovered.

Rail crossing, the area in which the Yankees created a "wagon park" on the old Spring Hill commons. (Photo Lochlainn Seabrook)

Cheatham's Corps, followed by Stewart's, crossed Duck River in Forrest's track, and, turning Schofield's left, marched toward Spring Hill, thirteen miles north of Columbia, where one brigade of Federals guarded a park of wagons [on the northwest side of town].

When General Stewart's column reached Rutherford's Creek, some miles below Spring Hill, he received an order from General Hood to halt his command and form a line facing the Columbia and Spring Hill Pike. This order was executed; and later he was ordered to resume his march toward Spring Hill. As he approached that place he encountered General Hood by a small fire on the roadside, with a single orderly as attendant. As soon as he came in speaking distance, General Stewart said, General Hood began to inveigh against Cheatham for not making the attack on Spring Hill, as he was ordered to do. General Stewart said to the writer:

> It was on my tongue to ask Hood, "Why did you not see yourself that your order was obeyed and the attack made?" but I thought that would appear disrespectful.

General Stewart said he asked General Hood why he had stopped his command at Rutherford's Creek, to which he replied that he thought Schofield might try to get out that way.

Hood had his whole army, including most of Forrest's command, except Lee's corps, assembled about Spring Hill and along the pike leading to Columbia during the afternoon and night, while Spring Hill was occupied by a small Federal force and Schofield was back at Columbia, confronted by General S. D. Lee. During the night Schofield marched his whole army from Columbia, through Spring Hill, passing along the pike in the immediate presence of Hood's army; and by morning was well on his way toward Franklin, with his whole wagon train practically intact.

In the writer's opinion General Schofield has never received due credit for the temerity displayed in making the attempt.

General Stewart further said that when he approached Franklin next day he again encountered General Hood, who was reconnoitering the enemy's position, and who asked him if he could cross the Harpeth River with his command, to which he replied that he was sure he could do so, as he knew there were fords on the river. He said he hoped that he would be ordered to cross the Harpeth and again turn the enemy's flank, saying that the mistake at Spring Hill would have been retrieved. But he was ordered to attack Franklin in front. The result the world knows was a bloody disaster.[34]
— T. G. DABNEY

## ON CONFEDERATE GEN. ALEXANDER P. STEWART

☛ Since the death [on August 30, 1908] of our regretted comrade, an incident about the Tennessee campaign at Spring Hill, Tenn., has come to light which we, the active participants in that memorable occasion, cannot allow to pass by in silence, the assertion by Gen. E. P. Alexander, chief of artillery Longstreet's Corps, author of *Military Memoirs of a Confederate: A Critical Narrative*, that Lieutenant General Stewart and General Cheatham, as rumored, had both that evening absented themselves from their divisions is, we assert most positively, false. We, as staff officers and courier to General Stewart on that eventful evening, declare that the General was most actively moving about enforcing General Hood's orders; that we never were within sight of the pike; that the sight we had of it was the next morning, when one of us prevented the Yanks from killing their mules with axes and from destroying the bridge.[35] — ARMY OF TENNESSEE VETERANS, C.S.A.

## MILITARY VIEW OF THE BATTLES OF SPRING HILL & FRANKLIN

☞ While pondering over these matters [I learned that] . . . General Schofield had not expected or planned for a battle at Franklin, as he was under orders from [Union] General [George H.] Thomas to continue his march from Spring Hill to Nashville, which he would have done had he found sufficient crossing of the Harpeth River. Disappointed at not being able to do this with celerity, he was forced to meet the sudden rush of Confederates [at Franklin, November 30, 1864]. His soldierly instinct taught him that a front attack upon his fortified position by advance over unobstructed and level ground for nearly two miles [as ultimately Hood ordered his troops to do] was not to be expected, and that a flank movement by crossing the river, which was fordable on the east, was the only proper course for Hood, so as by a wide circuit he might take the Federal army in the rear and cut off its retreat to Nashville, especially as he had successfully executed such a movement two days before at Columbia.

Spring Hill Cemetery, the resting place of numerous Confederate veterans, including several who died at the Battle of Spring Hill. (Photo Lochlainn Seabrook)

Accordingly Schofield in anticipation of this ordered one division of the 4th Corps, to be followed by others if necessary, to cross the river to the bluff on the north side. As a precautionary measure and for any emergency that might arise, he left General Cox with the 23rd Corps to hold the strong line of fortifications which had been hastily constructed and to resist any attack which might be made upon them, or in case of the flank movement to retire and join the forces upon the north bank; this, however, without any idea that an assault would be made from the front upon the heavily intrenched line. The fact that General Schofield did not expect this is evidence that Hood should not have made it. In the game of war, as in whist, never do that which your adversary wishes.

Hood's front movement [at Franklin] was made against the advice and protest of at least two of his generals, Cheatham and Forrest, the latter offering to undertake the flanking and promising to drive the enemy from his works on the north flank; and to do this he only asked a reasonable infantry support to his cavalry.

But stung into madness when he fully realized the golden opportunity he had lost the afternoon before at Spring Hill [November 29], Hood determined, despite the wise counsel of his commanders, to make the desperate attempt to retrieve his error by hurling his troops against the formidable intrenchments plainly in view. Rarely in the annals of war can there be a more forlorn attempt or a greater military blunder. It was Talleyrand who said of an error "that it was worse than a crime, for it was a blunder."

Had General Schofield the power to have directed a movement to destroy his assailants, he could not have done so more effectively ely than did General Hood. What followed is history, and it is needless to dwell upon the horrible details of the shambles of Franklin. In writing of it as regarding Cleburne's Division, General Hardee's words might well apply to that army: "It was there that Cleburne and his division found their graves."[36] — IRVING A. BUCK, C.S.A.

## PRESIDENT DAVIS ON THE BATTLE OF SPRING HILL

☞ Our army, as stated by President Davis, lost one of the golden opportunities of the war by failing to cut off the retreat of the enemy at Spring Hill. For this default of our army I forbear any criticism.[37] — JOHN M. BRIGHT, C.S.A.

## EVENTS LEADING UP TO SPRING HILL & FRANKLIN

☞ The Confederate army was in three departments: Army of Northern Virginia, Army of Tennessee, and the Trans-Mississippi. This latter department was not as conspicuous as the others until the closing events, when Lieut. Gen. R. Kirby Smith was promoted to general with temporary rank, and he had the concluding surrenders to make.

In Virginia, after the first year or so, Gen. Robert E. Lee was the only commander. He became dissatisfied with his services, and after the battle of Gettysburg sought to resign; but all the Confederacy opposed it, and President Davis positively declined to consider his retirement. Gen. Albert Sidney Johnston sought release from command of the Army of Tennessee (it was called the Army of Mississippi at the time he was killed) after the disasters at Forts Henry and Donelson and the evacuation of Tennessee. President Davis was equally as persistent in having

Jefferson Davis.

him remain in command; and so General Johnston, with the determination to win or die in the attempt, was successful to the very acme of victory, when in the providence of God his life was taken.

From that time there was much dissatisfaction with the commanders of the Army of Tennessee. Beauregard succeeded Johnston at Shiloh; then General Bragg was made commander with all the strength, moral and physical, that the President could give him. Beauregard failed to carry out the purposes of General Johnston and Bragg failed to followup the victory of his army at Chickamauga, and dissatisfaction resulted; then Bragg was succeeded by Gen. Joseph E. Johnston after the army had fallen back to Dalton and established winter quarters in 1863.

The campaign of 1864 began at Rocky Face Ridge, north of Dalton, early in May General Johnston had so reorganized and redisciplined that army as to restore confidence and create marvelous devotion to him by the soldiers. There was never in the history of wars doubtless an army that had more implicit faith in its commander than all had in General Johnston. His soldiers and his officers believed that everything he did was for the best. In the "hundred days' fighting" between Dalton, Atlanta, and on to Jonesboro the men believed whatever he did was the best possible, and somehow there was no doubt that in the end he would win. This condition of faith in Gen. J. E. Johnston could not be exaggerated to his army. Not so, however, at Richmond. Mr. Davis felt that he could not spare so vast a territory, and he was urged by many leaders in other sections to remove General Johnston, which he did when the army had fallen back to the Chattahoochee River, six miles north of Atlanta.

Gen. John B. Hood was appointed as Johnston's successor. The shock to the army was greater than ever befell it before the carnage at Franklin. Battles were fought and lost about Atlanta, and to meet a flanking force of Sherman's army at Jonesboro, twenty miles away, Hood sent a large part of his army there at night, and a disastrous battle occurred near Jonesboro the next day. Then the Confederate forces fell back to Lovejoy, five miles in the direction of Macon, and the Federals moved speedily there soon afterwards. Strangely, with the Confederate forces dreadfully depressed, Sherman ceased the pursuit and withdrew to Atlanta. Hood's forces returned to Jonesboro, and after some days moved across to Palmetto.

At that period the game of war was made up of startling events. President Davis came from Richmond, and on a memorable night, September 28, 1864, with wind blowing strong and flags fluttering over the pine-knot fires, he made a remarkable address to the army in which he gave the soldiers the plans that were to be followed, which were that the army would go into Tennessee for victory. Gov. Isham G. Harris and Gen. Howell Cobb also addressed the army, by which speeches much enthusiasm was aroused. It was great news to Tennessee soldiers especially.

As soon as practicable the army moved. Gen. B. F. Cheatham was put in command of Hardee's Corps, and Gen. John C. Brown was given command of Cheatham's Division.

Progress of the movement was as rapid, I assume, as practicable. The Federals holding the Western and Atlantic Railroad, the Confederate forces, west of it, moved north, attacking the Federals at Allatoona, where Gen. S. G. French with his division made a gallant fight at great disadvantage. Resaca was taken possession of, and largely during one night the Western and Atlantic Railroad track was destroyed for perhaps twenty miles extending to and north of Dalton. It was awfully hard work to loosen the rails, pile the ties, burn them, and across those fires heat the rails until they could be bent around trees and posts. A Colonel Johnson with a regiment of negroes in a very strong fort at Dalton persistently refused to surrender until General Cheatham, who demanded his surrender, assured him that not a man would be left alive if his men should be compelled to assault them in their works. Johnson finally surrendered without a fight.

Mark P. Lowrey.

During those days a part of Sherman's army was on its "march to the sea"—to Savannah, Ga.—while the remainder, perhaps two corps, were following Hood's army or paralleling it. A mysterious delay occurred when our army reached Tuscumbia and Florence. Delay of supplies was perhaps the unavoidable cause. However, there was inspiration in the march toward Tennessee, especially after reaching Mount Pleasant, which was on Saturday forenoon of November 27. That afternoon the army marched to the vicinity of Columbia, still occupied by the Federals. Sunday our army rested. On Monday morning, November 29, a large part of the army crossed Duck River a few miles above Columbia and marched along and across country roads, etc., in the direction of Spring Hill. It seemed so clear that the Confederates had stolen a march on Schofield that thrilling enthusiasm was created for General Hood.

Before sundown Cheatham's Division (commanded by Maj. Gen. John C. Brown) arrived at Spring Hill a little before sunset, and it was there that the private soldiers realized as they never did before the great importance of taking possession of the turnpike—and cutting off all of Schofield's army then south of Spring Hill. It was believed implicitly that that part of the army in the rear could have been captured.

Regiments and brigades were put in line of battle, and the men expected the command, "Forward!" every minute, but such command was not given. The Federals were in plain view between us and the setting sun. In great haste they piled rail fences for breastworks, while the officers, manifestly much excited, were galloping back and forth along their lines. The Confederates believed they could brush the enemy away and take possession of the pike. Still orders did not come, and after nightfall the soldiers began to build campfires, although the Federals were moving toward Nashville.

On Tuesday morning, November 30, the Confederate forces began to move north about sunrise along the pike toward Franklin. On that bright morning as the Confederate army moved this way from Spring Hill there was animation of spirit, and the soldiers remembered the banner at the crossing from Alabama, "Tennessee, a Grave or a Free Home." The movement of the troops was at quick step, but steady. The soldiers were cheerful as usual. Evidences of consternation with the enemy the night before tended to merriment.

I counted thirty-four abandoned wagons in a distance of seven miles of the march, and in a number of instances all the four mules had been killed; whether by Forrest's Cavalry or by the enemy to prevent capture, I could not learn.[38] [Later that day, Cunningham and his Confederate comrades entered the "Valley of Death" at Franklin, leaving nearly 2,000 Southerners dead on the battlefield by nightfall. L.S.] — SUMNER ARCHIBALD CUNNINGHAM, C.S.A.

## LEE'S CORPS: FROM COLUMBIA TO SPRING HILL

☛ Of the fatal blunders committed by the Confederates in the War between the States, the worst was—unless we except the removal of Gen. Joseph E. Johnston—when Hood left Georgia open to Sherman and took his own army into Tennessee. I was so impressed at the incipiency, and became more and more strongly so as the movement progressed. I gave this opinion to Generals Pettus and Pillow near Florence at the table of Mr. Patton, afterwards Governor of Alabama. That opinion doubtless became almost universal after the slaughter at Franklin, Tenn.

Stevenson's and Clayton's Divisions of Lee's Corps were left to confront Schofield at Columbia, while Hood with the rest of the army crossed the river a few miles above Columbia and placed himself in Schofield's rear at Spring Hill. Duck River approaches Columbia from a northerly direction, and on striking the hill upon which the town is built turns westward. The Federals upon leaving Columbia intrenched themselves upon the rising ground across the river. Their main line was more than half a mile from the river, the land sloping downward through an open wood from their intrenchments to near the river. Not far from the river they had a strong picket line in rifle pits. The enemy's attention was intentionally held through the day by constant firing from both artillery and small arms.

About 3:30 p.m. on the 29th of November, 1864, the 23rd, 31st, and 46th Alabama Regiments, under General Pettus, were run down the steep hillside in squads under a galling fire, sheltering under the river bluffs as they were put across the river in a pontoon boat. I went over the river with the first squad. As soon as the three regiments were over we were formed on the steep sides of the bluff. At the command of Pettus to [move] forward we rushed up the bluff, and some of the prisoners taken said it looked to them like we came up out of the earth. With a Rebel yell we dashed upon them, not heeding their sharp fire, and soon had possession of their line of pits and many of them prisoners.

The pursuit continued some distance toward the main line. My regiment, the 46th, was on the right next to the river as it approached the city. My men were enthusiastic, cheering as they rushed forward. A command to "halt!" came from General Pettus, which I repeated, but ran immediately to him, as he was only a short distance away, and said to him: "General, if you will let us go on, we can take their works, for they are getting out and hitching their horses to their guns." He ordered me with some sharpness to go back and halt the regiment. This was the only time in all the war that he ever spoke to me other than with kindness. He told me afterwards that he was in sympathy with my feelings, and believed himself that we could have captured their works, but that he had positive orders, twice repeated, to go no farther than

the picket line, and we were then considerably in advance of it. The result was that the enemy returned to their works and resumed fire with artillery and rifles, keeping it up till after night.

It was impossible to obtain any shelter for my men; so I ordered them to lie as close to the ground as possible. While so lying, doing nothing effective, I lost several of my best men, more, I am sure, than if we had gone on in the charge. When the command came to halt and I repeated it, some of the men shouted back, while their eyes flashed, one I remember in particular, Richards, a black-haired boy in his teens: "Halt! let's go on and take those works."

As soon as we had cleared the way the pontoon was laid, and a little after night the troops were crossing. We remained in line till all were across and formed, and then moved on after the fleeing foe, expecting to strike him in the rear while Hood held him in front. We expected nothing else but to bag the whole of Schofield's army.

There was no sleep for our two divisions that night, for it was all occupied in crossing the river, forming, and marching. When two or three hours had passed in marching, we were constantly expecting to hear the roar of battle; but no such sound greeted us. At last as it began to get light we came to Spring Hill, but there were neither Federals nor Confederates there. The campfires of the Confederates still burned along the pike but a short distance from it, along which the foe had walked almost unmolested through the trap well set for him. Why this was so has never been explained. It is a shameful puzzle yet, and will never be explained till time ends, for all who could make it have gone "over the river," not to return.

The Confederates had followed on upon the heels of the escaped foe and rushed upon him through broad, open fields as he lay sheltered behind his strong works at Franklin. Never was greater bravery and daring shown by soldiers than that of the army of Hood as it hurled itself in charge after charge against those death-dealing lines. The ground [at Franklin] was covered with the dead before, on, and over the works.

While the trenches were being prepared to bury the dead the next day (November 30) I walked along the line from the literally torn-up black locust thicket grove to beyond the pike road, and feel almost sure that I could have gone the distance by stepping each time upon the body of a dead soldier. I saw two, three, and in one instance four dead Confederates lying on or across each other. As many as thirty and even forty bullets had pierced some bodies. I counted seventeen dead Federals in the traverse across the turnpike. Our loss in killed was about three times that of the enemy. Six Confederate generals were killed, six wounded, and one captured.

Nothing was gained except reputation for bravery [at Franklin]. We reached the vicinity of Nashville later than if we had not fought. All this loss in men and loss of confidence in the commander depressed the spirits of our army, and perhaps accounts for some other things that took place afterwards. Fortunately for the two divisions of Lee's Corps, we were too late to take part in the blood-stained field of Franklin.[39] — GEORGE L. BREWER, C.S.A.

## WITH HOOD IN MIDDLE TENNESSEE

☛ . . . Hood crossed the Tennessee River at Florence, Ala., and moved in the direction of Middle Tennessee, capturing Columbia. He rested at Columbia one day, crossed the [Duck] river, marched to Spring Hill, Tenn., engaged the 4$^{th}$ Army Corps of Federal troops at that point, and bivouacked for the night.

Schofield's troops marched by on the pike from Columbia to Franklin unmolested, and, as General French wittily observed to Hood the next morning, "lighted their pipes at his bivouac fires on the side of the pike," and safely reached Franklin the next morning.[40] — DAVID WARD SANDERS, C.S.A.

## "IT SEEMED FATE"

☞ . . . General Hood was not so criticised for his defeats in battles around Atlanta as for his failure to fight at Spring Hill and then for the disastrous battle of Franklin, and again for waiting in front of Nashville for the organization of one of the largest armies in the history of that great war. [Most Confederate veterans have] never criticised General Hood out of sympathy mainly for his bodily afflictions [loss of a leg and a crippled arm]. [We recall] the spirit of the army on November 29, 1864, when it seemed certain that Schofield's army would be cut in two at Spring Hill and much of it captured. The inaction just at the most critical moment of the Army of Tennessee has never been explained, and may never be. It seemed fate.

Abraham Buford.

Private soldiers were dismayed, for it seemed that nine out of every ten of them could have ordered that army to victory. At Franklin General Hood evidently believed that he could crush the Federal forces and maybe get Nashville without a fight. The tragedy at Nashville, it may be, could not have been averted. It was evidently fatal to wait, and a more orderly retreat would hardly have succeeded. What a pity that General Hood did not quote General Lee after the defeat at Gettysburg and admit that "It was all my fault!"[41] — SUMNER ARCHIBALD CUNNINGHAM, C.S.A.

## ON HOOD'S CAMPAIGN TO FRANKLIN

☞ . . . I belonged to the 33rd Alabama Regiment, Lowery's Brigade, Cleburne's Division. . . . I don't know, but I think that after we crossed the Tennessee River at Florence, Ala., our line of march was straight through to Duck River, near Columbia, where we came to a halt on November 28. I lay quiet pretty much all the day; but just before night we marched up the river some distance and went in camp and stacked arms near the river bank. About dark a wagon was driven in front of our command and issued three ears of corn to the men.

The next morning, the 29th, we moved out in the direction of Spring Hill. Just before night we were drawn up in line of battle and moved forward, and soon were in sight of Spring Hill, where our cavalry had charged over a little ridge, fired, and fallen back. Our command relieved the cavalry, and drove the Federals back. We captured a number of their knapsacks that would average some fifty pounds each, and each one had a new pair of boots or shoes lashed on top.

Our command bivouacked in a skirt of woods near the pike leading from Columbia to Franklin. I suppose we were within eighty or one hundred yards of the pike. We could hear the Federal army tramp, tramp, tramp, moving on to Franklin. Some of our boys said the next morning that some Yankees straggled into our camp and inquired what command it was.

The next morning, the 30th, we were up early, called the roll, and struck out through woods, across fields, and waded creeks; but we got to Franklin all the same. . . .[42] — A. J. BATCHELOR, C.S.A.

## FORREST'S REPORT ON COLUMBIA & SPRING HILL

☞ . . . Columbia having been evacuated on the night of [November] the 28th [27th] I was ordered to move across Duck River on the morning of the 28th. Chalmers' division was ordered to cross at Carr's Mill, seven miles above Columbia, Jackson's, at Holland's Ford, while I crossed at Owen's Ford with a portion of Colonel Biffle's regiment. Before leaving Columbia I sent my escort to Shelbyville for the purpose of ascertaining the movements of the enemy and destroying the railroad, and I regret to announce that Captain Jackson was seriously wounded on this expedition.

On the night of the 28th I was joined by Chalmers' division about eight miles from Columbia on the Spring Hill and Carr's Mill road. Jackson's division was ordered to proceed to the vicinity of Hurt's Cross Roads on the Lewisburg pike. At 11 o'clock at night I received a dispatch from General Buford

Nathan B. Forrest.

informing me that the enemy had made such a stubborn resistance to his crossing that he could not join the command until the morning of the 29th. I ordered General Jackson to move along the Lewisburg pike toward Franklin until he developed the enemy. Brigadier-General Armstrong notified me that he had struck the enemy, when I ordered him not to press too vigorously until I reached his flank with Chalmers' division. The enemy gradually fell back, making resistance only at favorable positions.

After waiting a short time for my troops to close up, I moved rapidly toward Spring Hill with my entire command. Two miles from town the enemy's pickets were encountered and heavy skirmishing ensued. I ordered General Armstrong to form his brigade in line of battle. I also ordered a portion of the Kentucky brigade and the Fourteenth Tennessee Regiment, under Colonel White, to form, which being done I ordered a charge upon the enemy, but he was so strongly posted upon the crest of a hill that my troops were compelled to fall back. I then dismounted my entire command and moved upon the enemy. With a few men I moved to the left on a high hill, where I discovered the enemy hurriedly moving his wagon train up the Franklin pike. I ordered my command to push the enemy's right flank with all possible vigor. At the same time I ordered Brigadier-General Buford to send me a regiment mounted. He sent the Twenty-first Tennessee, Colonel Wilson commanding, which I ordered to charge upon the enemy. Colonel Wilson at the head of his splendid regiment made a gallant charge through an open field. He received three wounds, but refused to leave his command.

(Photo Lochlainn Seabrook)

About this time I received orders from General Hood to hold my position at all hazards, as the advance of his infantry column was only two miles distant and rapidly advancing. I ordered up my command, already dismounted. Colonel Bell's brigade was the first to reach me, when I immediately ordered it to the attack. Major-General Cleburne's division soon arrived, and, after some delay, was formed in line of battle and moved upon the enemy on my left. Colonel Bell reported that he had only four rounds of ammunition to the man when I ordered him to charge the enemy. This order was executed with a promptness and energy and gallantry which I have never seen excelled. The enemy was driven from his rifle-pits, and fled toward Spring Hill.

I then ordered Brigadier-General Jackson to move with his division in the direction of Thompson's Station and there intercept the enemy. He struck the road at Fitzgerald's, four miles from Spring Hill, at 11 o'clock, just as the front of the enemy's column had passed. This attack was a complete surprise, producing much panic and confusion.

Brigadier-General Jackson had possession of the pike and fought the enemy until near daylight, but receiving no support, he was compelled to retire, after killing a large number of horses and mules and burning several wagons. Chalmers' and Buford's divisions being out of ammunition, I supplied them from the infantry (my ordnance being still at Columbia), when I ordered Brigadier-General Chalmers to move at daylight on the morning of the 30$^{th}$ to the Carter's Creek turnpike, between Columbia and

Spring Hill, and there intercept a column of the enemy reported to be cut off. General Chalmers moved as ordered, but reported to me that the enemy had passed unmolested on the main pike during the night. . . .[43] —
NATHAN BEDFORD FORREST, C.S.A.

## CLEBURNE'S BRILLIANT IDEA: VETOED!

☛ I was not present at the Spring Hill affair nor at the battle of Franklin, being in prison at Fort Delaware, but have read General Hood's reports on the subjects and also the reports of several generals on both sides; also I have discussed both incidents with several Confederate officers participating therein, and especially with Gen. W. B. Bate and Gen. A. P. Stewart, both of whom were conspicuous at the two places.

I was present in General Bate's room at the Maxwell House with Gov. Isham G. Harris, Dr. Thomas Menees, and several others when General Bate gave a detailed statement of the Spring Hill affair. He said that his division, with General Cleburne's division, was ordered to cross Duck River above Columbia and intercept Schofield's army at Spring Hill; that his division was in advance and first got to the pike in advance of Schofield's army; that in a short while he received orders from his lieutenant general to fall back and rest on the right of the pike, and in reply thereto he reported that his division occupied a good position and could whip three times their number.

Soon thereafter General Cleburne, with his division, came up to the pike in his support; that about that time he received another order to fall back and rest on the right of the pike, and in reply he reported that Cleburne's Division had come up, was supporting him, and that the two divisions could whip all of Schofield's army; that he then received a peremptory order to fall back or to report under arrest to General Hood; that, knowing approximately where General Hood's headquarters were [Oaklawn], he secured two guides and ran his horse all the way there; that on arriving General Forrest was in the room with General Hood, and he was not invited in for several minutes; that when he did get in he told General Hood of the positions occupied by his and Cleburne's divisions; that General Hood asked him if Forrest's Division was not across the pike in advance of him; that he told him it was, but a division of cavalry could not stop an infantry army.

To this General Hood agreed, but after several minutes of contemplation he said: "You and General Cleburne had better obey orders, as your lieutenant general may have some move we know not of."

On getting back to his division General Bate ordered it from the pike. At this time General Cleburne came up and said: "Bate, suppose you and I report to General Hood under arrest and leave our divisions under the commands of our brigadiers, and before we can get back they will have whipped the Yankee army."

However, the divisions did fall back on the right of the pike, and in a very short time General Schofield and his army marched by and on into Franklin. Maj. H. J. Cheney, who was adjutant general of Gen. W. B. Bate at that time, and who now lives in Nashville, has read this paper and fully confirms every statement made.

Historical marker at the site of Forrest's successful attack on Yankee General James H. Wilson, near Spring Hill, TN. (Photo Lochlainn Seabrook)

Several years ago I was on the battle field of Chickamauga with the Commission to locate the positions for the placing of the Tennessee monuments and markers. On the Commission were a number of Tennessee Confederate officers, together with Generals Stewart and Bate, when General Stewart told of the attack upon Franklin. He said that soon after the Confederate army got in position in front of Franklin the officers held a conference, and he was ordered by General Hood to take his corps, with Forrest's Cavalry, and clear Harpeth River of the enemy above Franklin, so he with his army could flank Franklin and march into Nashville; that he did as ordered and so reported to General Hood; that soon thereafter he was ordered to attack Franklin, which was very much against his best judgment; that some time after the battle General Hood told him why he had changed his orders and did attack Franklin.

General Hood said he had information that the enemy were preparing to evacuate and hoped to strike them in a disorganized condition. It afterwards developed that Schofield had sent down to the river to see about evacuating, but found that the railroad bridge had no floor, and he could not take his army hurriedly across the river on crossties. Therefore he had given up his idea of evacuating just a short while before the attack was made.

. . . General Hood's report of the Spring Hill affair and General Bate's interview . . . contradict [all other explanations and theories of what occurred there]. General Hood knew that Schofield was in full and precipitous retreat, that his objective point was Franklin, and that he would not let his army stop until it reached there.[44] — JOHN P. HICKMAN, C.S.A.

## FORREST'S FRUSTRATION

☛ [Here is] what I know and saw of the operation of our army at Spring Hill. I was there on the staff of Gen. Abe Buford as inspector general of the division. General Forrest, with Buford's and Jackson's Divisions of Cavalry, was on the right flank of Hood's command and forced a crossing of Duck River several miles above Columbia. We found a good road from this crossing to Spring Hill, and we were nearer Spring Hill than Columbia was. Forrest at once sent a dispatch to Hood of this fact. At once Hood put his command in motion for a flank movement by this route. With his two divisions of cavalry Forrest at once moved on Spring Hill and struck the enemy at that place to cut them off; but they were too strong for us, and we were compelled to fall back.

Late that evening, just as the sun was setting, Buford's Division was in line of battle on their horses, about one-fourth of a mile, as nearly as I can recall, southeast of Spring Hill and about four hundred yards east of the road along which the Federals were retreating. Seeing a woman standing on the front porch of a neat cottage about one hundred yards in front of our line, I rode out and stopped at the gate, when she came out and joined me. I was struck by her great beauty, and began at once asking her about the roads and the lay of the ground.

After giving me the information, she asked what troops those were. I told her Buford's Division of Forrest's Cavalry. She at once asked if General Forrest was with us, and I pointed him out. She then said she would like to meet him and speak to him. I said, "Who are you, madam?" and she replied, "Mrs. Peters. General Forrest will know me."[45]

I, of course, knew her too, and immediately galloped back and told General Forrest that Mrs. Peters wished to see him. I took him to her and left them talking, and then rode forward about seventy-five yards nearer the Federal line of retreat.

Soon thereafter General Forrest joined me, and we sat on our horses for some time looking at the passing enemy. They moved back in a dense column across a valley in our front. At the same time there were quite a large number of pieces of their artillery stationed in front and near the Cheairs residence [Rippavilla] which had opened a heavy fire, throwing their shot and shells over the heads of their retreating army. I shall never forget General Forrest's expression. The longer he gazed upon this moving column, the madder he seemed to get, and finally he threw up a clenched fist and said: "Hood! Had he supported me here as he promised, that whole army would have been our prisoners." We finally rode back to our position and remained [there] far into the night.[46] — H. A. TYLER, C.S.A.

FROM A LETTER TO PRESIDENT JEFFERSON DAVIS
☛ . . . I have been with General Hood from the beginning of this campaign, and beg to say, disastrous as it has ended, I am not able to see anything that General Hood has done that he should not, or neglected anything that he should have done which it was possible to do. Indeed, the more that I have seen and known of him and his policy, the more I have been pleased with him and regret to say that if all had performed their parts as well as he, the results would have been very different.[47] — ISHAM G. HARRIS, C.S.A. (December 25, 1864)

Street sign named after Stephen D. Lee, Spring Hill, TN. (Photo Lochlainn Seabrook)

"THE GREAT MYSTERY OF THE WAR"
☛ It is almost universally admitted that if Hood had interposed Cheatham, Stewart, and Forrest across the pike at Spring Hill he would have trapped the Federals between those corps and that of S. D. Lee and would have captured them with all their trains of wagons and artillery. Hood's movements to this end were perfect, and his corps were commanded by officers who never refused to fight either before or after that time. They reached the proper position in due time to take the pike, but stopped in gunshot [range] of it and allowed all the Federals to pass practically unmolested. This is the great mystery of the war. A Union officer has written a book in which he mentions this occurrence as one among many other unaccountable accidents which prevented the ultimate success of the Confederacy, as if Providence had ruled that a fierce and bloody war should rage with high honors to the Confederacy, but ultimate success to the Union. Inexplicable things in the battles before Troy are detailed by Homer; a hero has another hero at his mercy, but Pallas interposes her shield and saves him—an easy explanation of an otherwise unsolvable denouement.

Testimony has been given on the Spring Hill affair by General Cheatham, General Hood, General Brown, Governor Harris, and others, and still there are great differences of opinion. No explanation in any way satisfactorily explains the inaction of that evening. Its dramatic effect is heightened by the fact that the bloodiest battle of the war was fought the next day at Franklin, twelve miles away. . . .[48] — PARK MARSHALL

# SECTION 2
# UNION RECOLLECTIONS

Although the precise number of Confederate soldiers who died at the Battle of Spring Hill is unknown, four who were known, Charles F. Waldman, Marcus L. Murdock, G. H. Jones, and John Bird, were buried in the Confederate section of Spring Hill Cemetery, along with a number of Confederates who perished the next day at the Battle of Franklin. (Photos Lochlainn Seabrook)

# UNION RECOLLECTIONS

John M. Schofield

## VIEW FROM THE TOP OF THE UNION CHAIN OF COMMAND

☞ ... Hood did not cross Duck River with his infantry in the night [of November 28, 1864], as had been expected, but Cleburne's division of Cheatham's corps, which was his head of column, crossed soon after daylight in the morning upon the pontoon bridge at Davis's Ford, followed by Bate and Brown. Stewart's corps came next, the rear being brought up by Johnson's division of Lee's corps, which was temporarily reporting to Stewart. Hood himself accompanied the advance guard, but despite all his efforts it was three o'clock in the afternoon, or later, when Cleburne reached the Rally Hill turnpike where it crosses Rutherford Creek, two and a half miles from Spring Hill.

Ordering Cheatham to remain and hurry the crossing of his other divisions, Cleburne was directed to press forward and attack whatever force there might be at Spring Hill, where the noise of Stanley's artillery warned them that Forrest was meeting with opposition. But the distant firing at Columbia could also be heard, and the tenacity with which Schofield hung on to the line of Duck River apparently raised doubts in Hood's mind whether the National commander might not have received reinforcements enough to cut boldly between the now separated wings of his army. Post's reconnaissance had gone far enough to observe the movement, and it is probable that it had in turn been seen by Hood's command, and he would thus know that infantry was approaching his line of march. But whatever the reasons which induced it, Hood ordered Stewart to form his corps in line of battle south of Rutherford Creek, facing west, and this instruction necessarily implies the expectation of the approach of an enemy from that direction, or the purpose of himself making an attack upon the line which Schofield had prepared to receive him by putting Wood's, Kimball's, and Ruger's divisions within supporting distance of each other upon the extension of Cox's left. He may have thought that the resistance at Spring Hill would be slight when Cheatham reached the field, and that this corps sweeping down the turnpike toward Columbia would meet the convergent advance of Stewart in a general attack upon Schofield's flank.

The advantages of the defence in a broken and wooded country, and the prudent disposal of his force, by which Schofield had now some miles of line facing the east, would possibly have made such an attack as disastrous as the one at Franklin next day; but Hood did not attack there, and Stewart remained in line till Cheatham had been repulsed at Spring Hill, and was then ordered up when darkness had fallen and it was thought too late for further action that night.

When Stanley had reached Spring Hill he found a part of Forrest's command already in the outskirts of the place. He ordered Wagner to put Opdycke's and Lane's brigades in position to cover the village, and advanced Bradley's brigade to a wooded hill about three-fourths of a mile east of the turnpike, which commanded the approaches from that direction. One battery of artillery had accompanied Wagner, but Captain Bridges, Chief of Artillery of the Fourth Corps, had followed Stanley's march with six batteries, leaving one with Wood's division. This had been done only to get them well forward en route to Franklin; but on reaching Spring Hill, Captain Bridges had with wise precaution put his guns in battery on a commanding bench just west of the road, and where a little later they proved of great use and most fortunate in position.

The enemy's cavalry made active efforts to reach the trains, which were parked by the roadside, and also to destroy the railway station a short distance west of the turnpike, and the protection of all these kept Opdycke and Lane fully employed. Bradley was engaged at the same time, but the affair was not serious until the arrival of Cleburne's division on the field. This officer formed his command along the Rally Hill road, and, advancing at right angles to it, attempted to reach the Columbia turnpike. He does not seem to have been fully aware of Bradley's position, for his extreme right (Lowrey's brigade) alone reached it, and was received with so rude a shock that Cleburne was quickly forced to change front nearly at right angles in order to engage his opponent.

Bate's division, which followed Cleburne, had formed in the same manner and took the same line of direction. It had nearly reached the Columbia road when Bate discovered that Cleburne had changed direction, and his orders being to form on the left of that division, much time was consumed in rectifying the line. Brown's division had followed Bate and had been sent forward on Cleburne's right. Bradley's position had been too isolated to be held by a single brigade against so extended a line of battle, and after his first sharp encounter with Cleburne he retreated in some disorder, he himself being severely wounded. The brigade was quickly reformed on the right of Lane, at the southern edge of the village commanding the Columbia road, and a regiment was detached from Opdycke to strengthen it.

Wayside exhibit, Spring Hill, TN. (Photo Lochlainn Seabrook)

Wagner's line was now a semicircle, reaching from the Columbia road around the eastern side of the place to the railway station on the northwest, Opdycke's brigade being stretched out till it was only a strong line of skirmishers. A regiment which was with the trains as a guard was also utilized, and advantage was taken of the ground to present the strongest front possible. Cleburne and Brown followed up Bradley's retreat, but were met with so continuous a fire and on so long a defensive line, that they were made to believe they were in the presence of a superior force. The concentration of artillery fire upon them was so far beyond what they could expect from a single division, that it checked them as much, perhaps, by producing the conviction that they had most of Schofield's army before them, as by the severe losses caused by the terrible fire of shrapnel and canister.

It was now growing dark, and Hood having reached the conclusion that he needed Stewart's corps also, ordered this up from Rutherford Creek, with Johnson's division of Lee's corps which accompanied it. Jackson's division of cavalry occupied Thompson's Station, three miles north of Spring Hill, and the rest of Forrest's horsemen were in that direction. When Stewart arrived it was already night, and he was ordered to bivouac on the right and rear of Cheatham.

Meanwhile Schofield had issued his orders that Cox's division should continue to hold the bank of the river opposite Columbia till nightfall, if possible, and then, leaving a skirmish line in position, should march to Spring Hill, followed in turn by Wood's and Kimball's divisions. The skirmishers were directed to remain till midnight unless driven off, and to join the rear guard of the army or follow it. The divisions were all to move by the left flank, so that whenever they should halt and face they would be in line of battle, and could use the road fences for barricades if attacked by Hood. The whole line would thus be shortened from the right till Kimball only should remain on that flank, when he also would march to Spring Hill. By this arrangement there was the least risk of confusion and the greatest readiness for any contingency which might arise.

On hearing from Stanley that he was attacked by infantry, Schofield hastened to Ruger's division, which, it will be remembered, was nearest to Spring Hill, and led its two brigades in person by a rapid march to Stanley's support. As he approached the village he found pickets of the enemy on the road, but these were driven off and he joined Stanley at seven o'clock. Whitaker's brigade of Kimball's division had also been ordered up, and followed Ruger closely. When it arrived it was placed on the right of Wagner's line, to cover the march of the rest of the column as it should approach. Learning from Stanley that some force of the enemy was at Thompson's Station, Schofield immediately marched with Ruger's division to that point to open the way to Franklin. At his approach Jackson withdrew his cavalry and Ruger was placed in position there without a contest. Schofield now returned to Spring Hill, reaching the village at midnight, and meeting there the head of Cox's division which had moved from Duck River in accordance with his orders.

It is necessary, to a complete understanding of the situation, that we should go back a little and notice the efforts which Lee made to carry out Hood's orders, and force the crossing of Duck River in the afternoon. He had kept up, at intervals, an annoying plunging fire upon Cox's troops in the bend of the river, but our rifled cannon, by greater range and better practice, had prevented the enemy's artillery from maintaining its positions or doing much damage. A line of skirmishers' pits on the very end of the tongue of land had been made untenable, but a fringe of wood, a little further back, afforded a cover which gave complete command of the open ground to the edge of the river bank. About four o'clock the efforts of Lee to effect a crossing became more energetic. Some pontoons were brought to the south bank of the river, and, under cover of a rapid artillery fire, a few boats were run down to the water. Some troops were ferried over in these, and so long as they remained under protection of the river bank, they could not be reached by our fire. As soon, however, as they appeared above its edge, and attempted to advance against the fringe of woods held by the Twelfth and Sixteenth Kentucky (part of Reilly's brigade) they were met by the most determined resistance. The Sixty-third Indiana and One Hundred and Twelfth Illinois, of Henderson's brigade (temporarily commanded by Colonel Stiles), were sent forward to support the right of Reilly's men, and the enemy was driven from the open ground to the cover of the river bank again, and made no further effort to cross the river during the evening.

An example of Confederate troops crossing a river over a pontoon bridge.

Soon after nightfall the line of pickets near the river was strengthened, the two Kentucky regiments, under command of Colonel White, were left as their support, the Division Inspector-General, Major Dow, being with them, and having orders to bring them off at midnight. The division then marched to Spring Hill, where it was directed by General Schofield to take the advance and proceed at once to Franklin, twelve miles further. The other divisions followed in the appointed manner and without serious interruption. The pickets at the river were withdrawn, as directed, and overtook the rear of Wood's division a little beyond Spring Hill, and, under orders from that officer, protected the flank of the trains from the cavalry of the enemy on the remainder of the march to Franklin.

Wagner's division was kept in position at Spring Hill till the trains and all the other troops were in movement, and Opdycke's brigade, which was the rear guard of the whole, did not march until six o'clock in the morning. About midnight Hood was informed that troops were passing on the Columbia road, and sent Johnson's division of Lee's corps to extend Bate's line and stop the movement; but the night was dark and the country unfamiliar, and nothing came of it but a slight occasional skirmish, while our columns marched by in full view of the enemy's camp-fires, which were burning less than half a mile away.

Here, as at Atlanta, Hood sought to shift the responsibility for his failure upon a subordinate, and Cheatham was now selected to bear the burden. Hood charged him with tardiness and weakness in the attack upon Stanley, and asked to have him relieved from his command. This request was withdrawn after the battle of Franklin, though without retracting the charge. But a commander who is personally with the head of column in such a movement and upon the field, has the means of enforcing his orders by direct commands to the divisions. Had his own confidence not wavered, and had he not begun to yield to the belief that much more than one division was before him, his own energy would have carried his subordinates with him, and would have made the assault as desperate, if need be, as it was next day.

But he seems to have lacked the grasp of mind which enables a general to judge and to act with vigor in the presence of circumstances which throw doubt upon his plan, and he proved inferior to his opponent in a strategic contest, which has been generally regarded as one of the most critical and instructive conjunctures of the war. The circumstances, as narrated by the leading Confederate officers who were present, show that Hood had an access of hesitation at the very moment when the success of his movement demanded that all doubts should be thrown to the winds and everything risked upon a desperate stroke.[49] — JACOB D. COX, U.S.A.

## UNION OPERATIONS AT SPRING HILL & HOOD'S FAILURES

☞ . . . General Hood had gone to bed in Thompson's house [Oaklawn] when he was informed that troops were marching along the pike. Without getting out of bed he directed Colonel Mason, his chief of staff, to send an order to Cheatham to advance on the pike and attack, but Mason admitted the next day, as stated by Governor Harris, of Tennessee, who was serving as a volunteer aide on Hood's staff, that he never sent the order. This strange neglect of the part of his own chief of staff affords a fitting climax to all the rest of the imbecility that contributed to Hood's failure after he had personally led the main body of his army to a position where by all ordinary chances success should have been certain.

There is a bit of Stanley's report that gives a clear glimpse of the situation as Schofield and Stanley believed it to be after they had met that night:

> General Schofield arrived from Columbia at 7 o'clock in the evening with Ruger's division. He found the enemy on the pike and had quite a skirmish in driving them off. My pickets had reported seeing rebel columns passing, east of our position, as if to get possession of the hills at Thompson's Station, and the anxious question arose whether we could force our way through to Franklin. It was determined to attempt this, and General Schofield pushed

on with Ruger's division to ascertain the condition of affairs.

Another vivid glimpse is afforded in the statement of O. J. Hack, a conductor on the railroad, who was also interested in a store at Columbia. He came down the road that day on the last train southbound, having in charge some goods for the store, and at the Spring Hill station met the last train northbound, and from the trainmen learned that the army was retreating. The two trains stood at the station that afternoon. Some time after dark, being anxious to save his goods, Hack went over to Spring Hill in quest of a guard to run the trains back to Franklin. On inquiring for headquarters he was directed to a large brick house where he found Schofield and Stanley together. Schofield, recently arrived from Duck river, had just been getting Stanley's account of the situation, and Hack said that Schofield was in a condition of great agitation, "walking the floor and wringing his hands." When Hack had told what he wanted, Schofield sharply replied that the enemy had possession of the road north of Spring Hill, and the trains could not move.

Emerson Opdycke.

The report of Stanley and the statement of Hack concur in showing that it was then Schofield's belief that Hood had possession of the Franklin pike; that the [Union] army was caught in a trap; that the only way out was the desperate expedient of forcing a passage by a night attack, and, failing in that, he must fight a battle next day under so many disadvantages that ruinous defeat, with the probable loss of the army, was staring him in the face. It would be interesting to know what Schofield then thought about his intimate knowledge of Hood's character, and his cool calculation based thereon, for which he afterwards so unblushingly claimed so much credit.

The two trains stood at the station until daylight was beginning to dawn when a detail of men came and began to build fires to burn the cars, but the detail was driven away, and the fires were extinguished before much damage was done, by the advance of the enemy. The two trains thus captured afforded the transportation to which Hood alluded in a letter to Richmond, written when he was in front of Nashville, wherein he stated that he had captured enough transportation to make use of the railroad in bringing up supplies. But Schofield ignored the loss of the two trains, for, in his official report, he explicitly states that with the exception of a few wagons, and of a few cattle that were stampeded, he arrived at Franklin without any loss.

When Schofield "pushed on with Ruger's division to ascertain the condition of affairs," on his arrival at Thompson's Station, three miles north of Spring Hill, he found camp fires still burning, but the brigade of cavalry that had been in possession there, withdrew without making any resistance. This very considerate action on the part of the cavalry was another of those lucky fatalities that so notably contributed to the escape of our army when such special fatalities were a vital necessity for its escape. After posting Ruger there to hold the cross roads Schofield returned to Spring Hill, where he arrived about midnight at the same time with the advance of Cox's division coming from Duck river. With this division he then hurried through to Franklin, picking up Ruger as he passed along, and thus saddling Stanley with all the risk of saving the artillery and the trains.

If they had been lost Stanley would have been the scapegoat, but with the same skill with which that afternoon he had bluffed off ten-twelfths of Hood's army with a single division, Stanley that night saved the artillery and the trains.

At 3 o'clock in the morning, when only a part of the trains had pulled out, the long column on the pike was brought to a standstill by an attack someplace in front. The situation was so critical that General Wood, who was then with Stanley, believing it would be impossible to save both troops and trains, advised that the trains be abandoned. But Stanley persevered until the attack was beaten off and the column again in motion. The two trains of cars had to be abandoned because a bridge had been destroyed north of the station, and about forty wagons were lost in the attacks made by Forrest between Thompson's Station and Franklin. Everything else was saved.

And, by the way, Stanley was one of the many good soldiers who were overslaughed by the big promotion obtained by Schofield. Stanley outranked Schofield, both as a captain in the regular army and as a major-general of volunteers, but by assignment of the President [Lincoln], gained by his extraordinary ability in the arts of diplomacy instead of by fighting ability displayed on the battlefield, Schofield was a department commander while Stanley was a corps commander, and it thus happened that Stanley was serving under his junior in rank.

Wagner's division was the last to leave Spring Hill. When night came Bradley's brigade began to intrench the line it was on, and kept at this work until nearly midnight when the men were called under arms, and spent all the remainder of that anxious, weary night on their feet. While standing in column we could hear to our left the rumble of the wheels while the artillery and the wagons were pulling out, and much of the time could be heard the dull tread of many feet and the clicking of accoutrements that told of the march of a column of troops along the pike, but there was no other sound—not even the shout of a teamster to his mules or the crack of a whip. All the surroundings were so impressive as to subdue the most boisterously profane men.

In expressing their dissatisfaction with the situation they were always careful to mutter their curses in a tone so low as to be inaudible a short distance away, for, looking to our right, we could see the glow on the sky made by the bivouac fires of the enemy, and in some places could see the fires with a few men about them cooking something to eat, or otherwise engaged, while most of their men were lying on the ground asleep. Every minute of those anxious hours we were looking for them to awake to the opportunity that was slipping through their fingers and grab hold of it by advancing and opening fire on the congested mass of troops and trains that choked the pike.

Historical marker on Columbia Pike, Spring Hill, TN., describing some of the events that took place on November 29, 1864, in the area. No mention of a "battle." (Photo Lochlainn Seabrook)

Occasionally our column would move on a short distance. Any orders that may have been given were spoken in a low tone at the head of the column. You would be apprised that the column was moving by the silent disappearance in the darkness of your file leader. You would hurry after him, and taking, perhaps, not more than a dozen steps, would be brought to a sudden halt by running against him, immediately followed by the man in your rear bumping up against yourself. Then would follow an indefinite wait until the column would again move on a short distance. The wearing suspense of the long waiting, while standing on our feet; the exasperating halts following those false starts, when everybody was almost frantic with impatience to go on; the excessive physical fatigue, combined with the intense mental strain when already haggard from much loss of sleep during the three days and nights preceding, make that night memorable as by far the most trying in nearly four years of soldiering. It afforded unspeakable relief when, just as daylight was beginning to dawn, our column finally got away in rapid motion for Franklin, the enemy dogging our heels with their close pursuit.

The location of Hood's headquarters was central as to the position of his troops until nightfall, and was, therefore, a proper one. But he was too far away to get any personal knowledge as to what was going on at Spring Hill, and he had to rely on the reports of his subordinates who were in contact with our troops. The character of those reports is unmistakably indicated by the second move that Hood made.

His first move . . . was based on the correct theory that a part of Schofield's army was at Spring Hill and a part at Duck river, and it contemplated thrusting in Cheatham's corps between those two parts. His second move, made after the fighting was all over, and he had received the reports of that fighting, was based on the theory that all of Schofield's army had reached Spring Hill, for, abandoning all purpose of cutting off any part south of Spring Hill, it contemplated seizing the pike north of Spring Hill and cutting off Schofield's retreat to Franklin.

Between sunset and dark, as stated by General Stewart, which would be about 5 o'clock at that season of the year, he received orders to cross Rutherford's creek with his corps, to pass to the right of Cheatham's corps, and to extend his right across the Franklin pike. After about five hours Stewart finally went into bivouac with his right more than a mile away from the Franklin pike. His explanations for his failure were the lack of a competent guide, the darkness of the night, and the fatigue of his men. To accomplish Hood's orders required a march of a little less than four miles by Stewart's head of column—about three miles by a direct country road leading into the Mount Carmel road, and the remaining distance across the country lying between the Mount Carmel road and the Franklin pike. It would seem that a guide might have been found among the cavalry who had explored the country that afternoon in developing the position of our line between the Mount Carmel road and the railway station, west of the Franklin pike; or there were men in some of the Tennessee regiments whose homes were in that vicinity, who were thoroughly familiar with the ground.

That no great difficulties were involved in the march is proved by the fact that Johnson's division made a similar march in about two hours, later in the night, to get into position on Bate's left. The night was as dark, the men were as tired, the distance was as great, and the way was as difficult for Johnson as for Stewart. In view of these plain facts it is a fair inference that Stewart made a very lukewarm effort to accomplish Hood's orders; that it was possible for him, by a display of no more energy than Johnson displayed, to have extended his right across the Franklin pike as early as 8 o'clock, and then when Schofield started north with Ruger's division about 9 o'clock, he would have found the way effectually barred.

The prime cause of Hood's failure was apparently the lack of confidence in his generalship on the part of so many of his subordinates. They had been dissatisfied with his appointment to the command of the army, and their dissatisfaction had been greatly increased by the failure of his attacks on Sherman's lines in front of Atlanta. With the poor opinion they held of Hood's ability it was not possible for them to give to any plan of his that wholehearted, unquestioning support that gives the best guarantee of success.

Simple as his plan was, they all failed to grasp the importance of getting possession of the pike and, Cleburne excepted, they all acted as if they were expecting a repetition of the disastrous experience that had followed the attacks on Sherman. The promptness with which Cleburne turned and rolled up Bradley's brigade when he was so unexpectedly assailed on his own flank, was the only energetic action on the part of any of them after they had crossed Rutherford's creek; and, no doubt, if Cleburne had not been halted by Cheatham's order, he would have gone on until he had reaped the full measure of success made so easily possible by the faulty situation of our army. But amid all the exciting occurrences of that eventful evening it is amazing that no inkling of that faulty situation seems ever to have entered the mind of any one of those veteran generals.

David S. Stanley.

Hood made a mistake, as stated by himself, in not taking Lee's corps on the flank march instead of Cheatham's corps. He believed that with Lee in Cheatham's place he would have succeeded, and in view of the skill with which Lee executed the part assigned to him to hold Schofield at Duck river, it is more than probable he would have given at Spring Hill far better support than Cheatham gave. Hood led Cheatham within sight of an easy and brilliant success, and it was the hesitation displayed by Cheatham, Brown and Bate at the critical time, that defeated Hood's plan and saved Schofield's army. That their hesitation was not due to any lack of courage on their part, or on the part of the troops they commanded, was abundantly proved by the unsurpassed courage with which they assaulted at Franklin next day when it was everlastingly too late. If they had fairly utilized at Spring Hill one-tenth part of the courage that was thrown away on the breastworks of Franklin they would have changed the later current of the war with results too far reaching to be estimated.

The prime purpose of Schofield's campaign was to delay Hood. How well he succeeded in that purpose can be significantly stated in a single sentence: The evening of November 29$^{th}$ he was at Duck river, and the morning of December 1$^{st}$ he was at Nashville, more than forty miles away. Then followed the panicky feeling displayed by the [Lincoln] Administration, and by General Grant, because General Thomas was not ready to attack Hood immediately on his appearance in front of Nashville. If Schofield's orders at Duck river had been to make no effort to delay Hood but to get inside the fortifications of Nashville with the least possible delay, he would not have covered the distance in so short a time without the spur of Hood's flank movement, and the celerity with which he ran out of the country was due to the scare he got at Spring Hill.

From Franklin next day he wired General Thomas at Nashville that he had come through, but that the least mistake on his part, or the fault of any subordinate, might have proved fatal, and he did not want to get into such a tight place again; that a worse position for an inferior force than the one at Franklin could hardly be found; that he had no doubt Forrest would be in his rear next day, or doing some worse mischief, and that he ought to fall back to Brentwood at once.

In short, his Franklin dispatches, read by the light of Stanley's report and of Hack's statement, clearly show that his mind [Schofield's] was still dominated by the fright of Spring Hill, and that he could feel no security short of Brentwood, where he would be backed up too close to Nashville for Hood to have room to repeat that terrible flank movement. Not even the wrecking of Hood's army on the breastworks of Franklin that evening could reassure Schofield. He insisted on retreating to Nashville that night when thousands of the men were in such a condition from more than forty hours' of incessant marching, fortifying and fighting that they dozed on their feet while they were walking, and in spite of the manly protest of General Cox, who was so urgent in his efforts to persuade Schofield no more running was necessary, that he offered to pledge his head he could hold the position.[50] —
JOHN K. SHELLENBERGER, U.S.A.

THE "OTHER SIDE" AT SPRING HILL
☛ I was a member of what was known as Casement's Brigade, Twenty-Third Army Corps, U.S.A.

We had been on the Atlanta campaign during the spring and summer of 1864, having begun at Rocky Face Ridge, near Dalton, Ga., and finished up that campaign September 2, when Hood abandoned Atlanta. After a month's rest at Decatur, Ga., we marched back to Allatoona, Ga., and compelled French to let go there, when he had Corse penned up and was threatening our "cracker line." After this event it was sure that Hood had a northern campaign in view. He had made up his mind to let Sherman go, and he would make a break for the North, as Bragg did in 1862. We then left Georgia and were transferred to Pulaski, Tenn., to confront Hood.

We arrived there November 20, 1864. There was nothing worthy of note at this point.

In a day or two we began to retire on Columbia, stopping at Lynnville one day. While there we learned that Forrest was threatening Columbia from the west on the Mount Pleasant Pike. We struck tents and marched out for Columbia, our brigade in the lead. We made that march of fifteen miles without a halt in just four hours, and arrived at Columbia just in time to save Capron and his brigade of cavalry, as Forrest was pressing him very hard.

(Photo Lochlainn Seabrook)

We formed a line of battle directly across the Mount Pleasant Pike. Our battery came up, unlimbered, and with a few well-aimed shells served notice on Forrest that he was up against the "real thing"; that he had both infantry and artillery in his front. We deployed a heavy skirmish line and went out and relieved our cavalry and had a hot skirmish with Forrest ourselves that evening and the next day.

That was our debut in the Hood Tennessee campaign. We held that line two days, I think, and on the night of the 26$^{th}$ we crossed to the north side of Duck River and hung on there, expecting Thomas to send us reenforcements sufficient to warrant us in making the big fight there, but they came not; and as Hood kept pressing us closer each day, it became evident to Schofield that we had to move again. So on the 29$^{th}$ Schofield began sending his trains to the rear under strong guard.

A little later he began to send the artillery and some infantry to the rear, but we still hung on to our line along the river bank. About five o'clock we could hear the artillery booming in the distance, in the direction of Spring Hill. About that time our brigade was pulled out of line and started toward Spring Hill; and, after marching about three miles, our regiment was taken out of the column and was placed as pickets on the cross roads or trails that run from the Columbia Pike to the road that Hood's troops were on, headed for Spring Hill as fast as they could march.

From where we were in the woods we could hear the familiar "chuck" of Hood's artillery as it was urged along the road. We could hear very plainly the artillery firing at Spring Hill. We held our position in the woods until the firing had ceased at Spring Hill and all was quiet, except the "chuck" of Hood's artillery and wagon train.

About ten o'clock that night we were much pleased by receiving orders to retire to the Franklin Pike and report at Franklin in the morning if possible. In a few minutes we were on the pike and headed for Franklin. We passed through Spring Hill just before midnight. Just before coming into this town we came within plain view of Hood's army as they were in bivouac to our right, not more than half a mile. They had thousands of fires burning brightly, and we could see the soldiers standing or moving around the fires. It was a rare and grand spectacle to behold. We were only one company of thirty-five men passing right through Hood's army. The view was grand, the feeling intense; but we "kept to the middle of the road," and hustled along toward Franklin. We reached Spring Hill all right, and found Wagner's Division of the Fourth Corps there.

Then we felt pretty good, but were disappointed at not finding our regiment there. They had been gone two hours, and were away on their march to Franklin, leaving word for us to follow on if we were lucky enough to reach Spring Hill. So, after getting our wind, a drink of water, and tightening our belts to suit present conditions, we moved out into the night and on our way to Franklin.

As we neared Thompson Station we came on to a small wagon train that had been attacked by a squadron of cavalry. Some of the teamsters had cut the traces of their teams and had ridden away; others had stuck to their train. As soon as we arrived on the scene we opened up on the cavalry with our rifles, and soon had them going. We could hear them ride away in the darkness. We straightened out what was left of the train and hustled them off toward Franklin. I think there were about twenty-five to thirty wagons abandoned there. We fell into the road again and continued our march. Soon after leaving Thompson Station we met Gen. Schofield and staff coming back from Franklin. He was anxious as to his rear, and had ridden back personally to see how things were going. A staff officer addressed us, asking who we were and what we had seen as we were coming into Spring Hill. In the meantime Gen. Schofield rode up and began asking questions, and when we told him we had seen a large army in bivouac, he expressed pleasure and said it was good news to him, as he would not be troubled any more that night. He said: "Your command is many miles in advance of you, and you had better hurry on. You will find them at Franklin."

So on we went; and, as nothing happened to us on our way, we just kept hitting the pike the rest of the night, and about eight o'clock in the morning we arrived at our lines, near the Carter House, at Franklin. There we found our command.

That night march from Columbia to Franklin will never be forgotten by me. We made at least twenty-two miles of the distance in company with only thirty-five men. It was a very lonesome, weary march, and while we were passing along the road in plain view of an army corps of Hood's army it was a little exciting, I assure you.

In my narrative we are now at Franklin. It was a beautiful November morning. The sun rose bright and glorious. There was nothing to suggest that we were standing on a spot that was soon to become historic; that the action that was to take place there in a few short hours was to make some names immortal, and many others were to be written well up toward the top of the temple of fame. Little did we think that so many of the bravest of the brave were to end their earthly careers there, many who were veterans since Shiloh, who had passed through the fire of Vicksburg, Chickamauga, Mission Ridge, Resaca, Kennesaw, Peach Tree, and Atlanta. They seemed almost immune; yet they were to be cut down as stalks before the sickle and blown away from the muzzles of the guns as chaff before the wind.

Though Edwin Forbes made this sketch of Union soldiers in the Eastern Theater, it closely matches descriptions of the "rare and grand spectacle" at Spring Hill on the night of November 29th and early morning of the 30th, 1864, when Yankee troops quietly rode past "thousands of [Confederate] fires burning brightly" in the hills above town. This "lost opportunity," which helped lead the Federals to victory in April 1865, continues to haunt *and* affect the South to this day. (Drawing circa 1876.)

. . . As to any criticism on the great battle of Franklin, I will say but little. Hood failed to press his advantage at Spring Hill. Schofield had to stop at Franklin in order to save his wagon train. Hood sought to retrieve the lost opportunity of the day before and by one grand, supreme effort to destroy Schofield's army before he could retire on Nashville and unite with

Thomas. Had Hood succeeded, he would have received the plaudits of the world, and his name and fame would have been perpetuated in song and story for ages.[51] — TILLMAN H. STEVENS, U.S.A.

## A NOTE FROM A YANKEE SOLDIER TO CONFEDERATES
☞ My division had the "scrap" with Hood's army at Spring Hill on the 29th [of November 1864], and was rear guard from Spring Hill to Franklin. . . . That was a critical conjuncture at Spring Hill when four divisions of the Federal army passed the Confederate bivouac, disturbing Johnson's picket line near the Columbia pike. A number of our stragglers are reported to have penetrated your camp, supposing our troops had gone into camp for the night, and, on finding their mistake, to have resumed their tramp without asking for lodgings with you or bespeaking your hospitality.[52] — W. D. THOMPSON, U.S.A.

## HOOD'S DEFEAT AT SPRING HILL & FRANKLIN
☞ Maj. Gen. Stanley, commanding the Fourth Federal Corps, in his official report, stated:

> In view of the strong position we held, nothing appeared so improbable as that they would assault. I felt so confident in this belief that I did not leave Gen. Schofield's headquarters until the firing commenced.

Maj. Gen. Cox, commanding the Twenty-Third Corps, and in active command of the Federal line of battle, undertakes to account for the attack made by Gen. Hood thus:

> His exasperation at what he regarded as a hairbreadth escape on our part from the toils in which he thought he had encompassed us at Spring Hill had probably clouded his judgment. He blamed some of his subordinates for the hesitation which he seems himself to have been responsible for, and now, in an excitement which led him astray, he determined to risk everything upon a desperate assault [at Franklin the next day, November 30, 1864].

The same eminent author, referring to the assault made by Cleburne and Brown on the Federal center [at Franklin], says: "They were seen coming in splendid array. The sight was one to send a thrill through the heart, and those who saw it have never forgotten its martial magnificence."[53] — UNKNOWN

## HOOD'S MANY ERRORS
☞ Our brigade [Opdycke's Brigade, Co. C., 88th Illinois Volunteer Infantry, 2nd Div., 4th Corps] was rear guard from Spring Hill to Franklin [where we fought Hood on Wednesday, November 30, 1864]. . . . The

(Photo Lochlainn Seabrook)

opportunity of Hood was lost when he let us get by him at Spring Hill. There was his chance, and he failed to improve the opportunity. The hearts of Hood's men were broken when the survivors the next morning [Thursday, December 1] scattered over the battlefield [at Franklin] and looked upon the faces of over seventeen hundred dead. That was the reason Hood's army did such poor fighting at Nashville a few days afterwards [December 15-16, 1864]. [Confederate] Col. [Hiram M.] Bledsoe, a resident until he died at Pleasant Hill, Mo., commanded Bledsoe's Battery in that battle. He told me where he was stationed. If so, it was his battery who killed many of their own men in that battle, as cannon balls plowed through their own ranks from the rear and struck the front of our works. He told me as late as 1880 that he told Gen. Hood he was firing on their own men, and that Gen. Hood told him he was mistaken and to keep on firing; but I know he was right.[54] — J. K. MERRIFIELD, U.S.A.

ANOTHER YANKEE OBSERVATION
☛ The question has often been raised: "Why did General Hood fight that battle [at Franklin]?" . . . If Hood had made an attack on us at Spring Hill, in my opinion a different tale would have been told, and the Northern army would have been routed; and if Hood had succeeded in breaking our lines at Franklin, he would have captured or killed all troops south of the [Harpeth] river and would have come on into Nashville.[55] — J. K. MERRIFIELD, U.S.A.

THEORIES & RUMORS
☛ Another account [concerning the Confederate failure at Spring Hill] indicates that, with all the rage that Hood showed afterward at his lost opportunity, he had himself an access of irresolution. Gen. Bate reports that on that night he had occasion to go to the headquarters [Oaklawn], which were about two miles back from the road, and there found Hood in consultation with General Forrest, at the conclusion of which he turned to Bate and said that no movement would be undertaken that night; for that Forrest had just reported to him that he could easily seize and hold the pike at a point above Spring Hill, which would prevent the passage of Schofield, so that in the morning "they would bag the whole Federal army"!

While thus vindicating the good name of his old friend, the Major [Joseph] Vaulx takes occasion to stamp out another cruel story which has been permitted to float about in different quarters. As if the imputation of unmilitary conduct in disobedience of orders, were not enough, the charge is made still more odious by the explanation given of this culpable neglect, viz: that General Cheatham was grossly intoxicated! This I myself have heard stated, not as a mere rumor, an idle report, but as something which "everybody knew" in the army. To this Major Vaulx gives a peremptory denial. He says:

> I was with Gen. Cheatham when he was giving his orders to Gen. Brown. The charge that he was intoxicated is false. I never saw him more self-possessed than on that afternoon. He gave his orders in a very plain and explicit manner. His words expressed just what he wanted, and in such a manner that no doubtful construction could be given them.

To the same effect, ex-Governor Porter of Tennessee writes:

> I was with Cheatham during the entire day from Columbia to Spring Hill, and he was not only not intoxicated, but I am positive that he did not taste nor see a drop of liquor of any kind.

The injustice of a Commander-in-Chief [Hood] throwing upon a subordinate a responsibility which he should take upon himself, is answered by the Major with this telling remark:

> General Hood was himself on the field, but a few hundred yards from Cheatham's line, and if he felt that his orders were not being obeyed, he could have ridden to the front in five minutes, and in person ordered the charge which he blames Cheatham for not making.

Major Vaulx adds these further particulars:

> Gen. Edward E. Johnson's Division was detached from Stephen D. Lee's Corps, then at Columbia, and arrived in front of Spring Hill after dark. Gen. Johnson was ordered by Hood to report to Cheatham, and Hood ordered Cheatham to have Johnson placed in position to command the turnpike road running from Columbia to Spring Hill. Gen. Cheatham sent his Staff Officer, Major Joseph Bostick, to order Gen. Johnson to take such a position (Johnson had gone into bivouac). Upon getting this order, Johnson vehemently objected to undertaking this movement in the dark; said he could not do it, as he had no idea of the country, or the position of the other troops; that he had reached the ground after dark, and knew nothing about directions; and if he went to moving about in the dark, he would be liable to run into some of our own troops, and they would fire into each other.
> Major Bostick suggested that he could show Gen. Johnson where the turnpike was, and point out where our lines were posted; but Johnson said he could not, and was not willing to undertake such a movement in the dark, ignorant as he was of the country and all surroundings. It was then suggested by Major Bostick that he had no decision in the matter, but that Gen. Johnson might give orders to his command to prepare to move, and then go himself

to Gen. Cheatham, and lay the case before him, which he did, and impressed it upon Gen. Cheatham that he could not undertake the move intelligently or safely.

But the next morning, when Hood found that the great opportunity had been lost, he was unwilling to bear the reproach of its being due to any want of energy on his own part.

. . . Aside from this Confederate testimony, it argues a certain simplicity in the commander of an army to assume that, while he is wide awake and urging on his soldiers, the opposing commander is not equally vigilant and equally determined. The whole argument of Hood seems to imply that the Union commander was quite unprepared, whereas General Schofield had had his eyes open all the time to the possibility of such a flank movement, and as soon as the cavalry reported that the enemy were crossing the river, he at once despatched General Stanley with a division comprising three brigades and all the reserve artillery of the Fourth Corps to Spring Hill, with orders to throw up intrenchments and hold the position.

(Photo Lochlainn Seabrook)

As these bickerings between Gen. Hood and his corps and division commanders contributed so much to defeat the Confederate army, they suggest by contrast the opposite state of things in the Federal camp, where General Schofield was supported by Generals Stanley and Cox, on whom he relied with the absolute confidence that one brave man gives to another. The situation was critical. The Union army was threatened on two sides: by the flanking movement directed towards Spring Hill, and at the same time by the persistent attempt to force a passage of the [Duck] river at Columbia, where the attack was kept up without intermission.

Had Schofield withdrawn his whole force, the Confederates would have immediately crossed with all their heavy artillery, which could have been transported rapidly over the hard, macadamized turnpike. Against both these movements, aimed at points ten miles apart, he had to be equally prepared. As has been well said, "He must hold back his enemy at Columbia with one hand, and fend off the blow at Spring Hill with the other."

So while Stanley marched with all speed to Spring Hill, Cox was ordered to hold on to the last moment at Columbia, to prevent the enemy crossing the river. It was to the admirable manner in which both these orders were carried out, that was due the success of this and the following day.[56] — REV. HENRY MARTYN FIELD, NEW ENGLAND AUTHOR

Part of the Spring Hill Battlefield at Rippavilla. (Photo Lochlainn Seabrook)

Rippavilla, built by Nathaniel F. Cheairs, the author's 4th cousin, Spring Hill, TN. On November 30, 1864, the morning after the "Spring Hill Affair," Hood and his officers met here for breakfast, where they argued bitterly about the events of the previous day. Afterward they rode north on the Columbia Pike (modern Highway 31) to meet their fate on the open fields of Franklin. (Photo Lochlainn Seabrook)

# SUMMARY

## By Colonel Lochlainn Seabrook

W E HAVE READ THE WORDS of dozens of both authoritative Confederate and Union officials, most who were eyewitnesses at the Battle of Spring Hill. Many are contradictory; some are baffling; a few are altogether enigmatic. Bizarrely, the movements of both armies that day were sometimes odd, overly risky, and unaccountable when one considers the hilly terrain, the potentially "fateful consequences," and the astonishing disparity of numbers (25,000 Confederates against 7,000 Yankees) that were involved.[57] Indeed, massive blunders were made on both sides, by officers and by their two commanders (both Schofield's and Hood's men, for example, considered some of the orders they were given "strange"). It is almost as if a weird fog benumbed the minds of those in charge during that 24-hour period, causing them to behave unusually and even abnormally. "It seemed fate," mystically commented one Confederate veteran later.

Battle of Spring Hill site, showing general location of tollgate (on road in back)—often mentioned by the participants. (Photo Lochlainn Seabrook)

And yet, it is not the Union's many mistakes and misdoings at Spring Hill that people focus on. It is the Confederacy's. This phenomenon we must chalk up, in great part, to the fact that the North is considered the victor.

Because the Battle of Spring Hill took place in the South, in a Confederate town, in a Confederate county and state, and because my relatives were wearing Confederate gray on the meadows of Maury County that day, our own focus too has been on the Confederate side of things. For us here in the traditional South, it is the more interesting and important side after all!

What is one to make of the Confederate's striking loss at the Battle of Spring Hill? Who was responsible for the fiasco that led up to it? After studying the War for Southern Independence for over 40 years and writing some 45 books on the subject, many have been interested in my opinions on the matter.

While subordinate Confederate officers certainly played a role of one kind or another at Spring Hill, ultimately the responsibility for whatever occurred there must fall on the shoulders of the gallant if sometimes ineffectual General John Bell Hood; just as General Robert E. Lee was responsible for the Confederate loss at Gettysburg—whether he was actually to blame or not. As has been pointed out, the difference between Lee and Hood is that the former accepted this fact, the latter did not.

What could General Hood have done differently?

To be certain the job got done, he could have personally led his men into battle, as Forrest and many other Confederate officers often did throughout the War. And yet, Hood was severely crippled (the one-legged officer had the use of only one arm, and had to be lifted and strapped onto his horse), making this impossible.

I believe that what he actually should have done is this: instead of going to bed amidst confusion over competing orders and inconsistent statements regarding the movements of the Yankees, Hood could have remained awake through the night and taken personal control of the situation as it unfolded, ensuring that the Union march through Spring Hill was halted and Schofield's army destroyed. Nearly all of Hood's officers maintained that the Federals could have been easily stopped at Spring Hill: *if the Confederates had only acted decisively and in concert*. If they had, the tragedy at Franklin the next day (November 30, 1864) would have been averted, and the Confederate rout at Nashville two weeks later (December 15-16, 1864) would have almost certainly been avoided as well. Instead, in a mere 35 days, from his start in Georgia, Hood's military policies nearly decimated the 51,000-man Army of Tennessee, the mightiest Confederate power in the Western theater, helping, in turn, guarantee Lee's surrender to Grant only months later.[58]

Prelude to Spring Hill; historical marker, Mt. Pleasant, TN. (Photo Lochlainn Seabrook)

So what really happened at Spring Hill? Why did the Confederacy not attack under perfect conditions, wasting the best opportunity Hood's army would ever have to save the heart of the Confederacy, Middle Tennessee, and ultimately the South herself?

Many theories have been proposed, all which probably contain a grain of truth: Hood was unqualified for his position; the officers did not like Hood and resisted his orders; Hood was mentally sluggish from taking laudanum (a tincture of opium) or drinking whiskey to ease the pain of his injuries; the list goes on. Yet, none answer the question satisfactorily. Not even the officers involved ever agreed on the cause. In fact, most stated that it was a jigsaw puzzle that could never be put back together.

Thus, as it stands, we are left with an unsolvable conundrum. Many of the Confederate officers who might have known what happened at Spring Hill were killed the next day at Franklin, and by the very Yankees whose lives they had unwittingly spared the day before. Those Spring Hill servicemen who survived the War disagreed on major points, their testimonies conflicted on various significant aspects, their eyewitness accounts often differing considerably. As these dauntless Southern veterans passed one by one into their final rest throughout the late 1800s and early 1900s, they left no definitive answers, no consensus on the cause of what took place November 29, 1864. And thus one early Southern writer variously described the "Spring Hill Affair" as an "unaccountable accident," an "inexplicable thing," an "unsolvable denouement," and most accurately and dramatically, "the great mystery of the War."

Cheairs family cemetery, Spring Hill, TN. This area was within the Confederate lines on November 29, 1864. (Photo Lochlainn Seabrook)

Yet, one thing nearly everyone agreed on was where the final guilt of the Confederate calamity lay. And that was with Hood—whether he technically truly deserves that dubious distinction or not.

For Southern historians like myself, the Spring Hill disaster, fascinating as it is to study, leaves us with a long list of "if onlys": if only communication between Hood and his men had been more forthright; if only there had been less contention and more good will among the commanders; if only high-level officers in the field had been given more freedom to act on their own accord; if only Cleburne's ingenious idea had been used; if only Forrest had been given command of the Army of Tennessee instead of Hood!

Whatever one's view of the War for Southern Independence, all honorable people believe that the Confederate soldiers who fought, bled, and died at the Battle of Spring Hill deserve recognition, and that means the erection of a town monument in their name; a eulogy in stone that commemorates the bravery, patriotism, and heroism of Hood and his men in the face of nearly irresistible odds, for Lincoln's combined U.S. forces possessed three or four times the manpower and firepower as the South, and nearly unlimited funding.⁵⁹

The Confederate soldiers at Spring Hill took up arms not to "preserve slavery" or to "destroy the Union," as our mainstream history books falsely claim.⁶⁰ As Southern Conservatives they fought, as they themselves energetically asserted time and time again, to preserve the original government and Constitution of the Founding Fathers, which included the tacit promises of states' rights, self-government, and individual freedom. This is the same foundation upon which modern conservatism is built, for today's Conservatives are the political descendants of Confederate men and women.⁶¹

This is why it was not the South that lost at Spring Hill. It was America! For the government of the Founding Generation was severely eroded by the Liberal victors after the Civil War, and ever since, Conservatives have been spending every waking moment trying to preserve what is left of it.⁶² Do not the Spring Hill Confederates, who fought to uphold the Founders' values, deserve to be memorialized in stone for their courage and patriotism? Have they not earned the right to be remembered, to have their Americanism honored and their names celebrated? Their modern political descendants, traditional Southerners, says yes.⁶³

I can do no better than to close my little book on the Battle of Spring Hill with the words of one of the great Conservatives of the 19ᵗʰ-Century: Tennessee native and Confederate veteran Sumner Archibald Cunningham, founder of that noble and important periodical, *Confederate Veteran*. Speaking on November 30, 1909, in honor of the 45ᵗʰ anniversary of the Battle of Franklin, Cunningham's words are just as applicable to both the Battle of Spring Hill and to the intrepid patriots who risked and even sacrificed their lives there the day before:

> This brief and very inadequate account of the battle has been printed for complimentary distribution in the hope that the greater interest be aroused among all the people of Franklin that they will always celebrate this day and cooperate in every practicable way to have the battle area preserved and suitably marked as the spot on which American valor was unexcelled.
>
> In what I have said concerning dissatisfaction with generals in command I would not be understood as justifying complaints. There were grave mistakes made, but the ability and the faithfulness of Confederate generals are a source of pride and gratitude to which we should cling for all time. Even at Spring Hill, where the greatest of misfortunes occurred, I have no word of reproach.⁶⁴

*The End*

# NOTES

1. Woods, p. 47.
2. On Lincoln's socialistic, Marxist, and communist thoughts, ideas, and tendencies, see my books: *Lincoln's War: The Real Cause, The Real Winner, the Real Loser*; *Abraham Lincoln Was a Liberal, Jefferson Davis Was a Conservative: The Missing Key to Understanding the American Civil War*; *Abraham Lincoln: The Southern View*. Also see McCarty, passim; Browder, passim; Benson and Kennedy, passim.
3. See J. W. Jones, TDMV, pp. 144, 200-201, 273.
4. See Seabrook, TAHSR, passim. See also, Pollard, LC, p. 178; J. H. Franklin, pp. 101, 111, 130, 149; Nicolay and Hay, ALCW, Vol. 1, p. 627.
5. For more on the nihilistic, atheistic, anti-life, anti-tradition, anti-American, anti-Constitution, anti-capitalism, anti-South agenda of the Victorian Republican Party (then the Liberal Party) and the modern Democrat Party (now the Liberal Party), otherwise known as "The Communist/Socialist Rules for Revolution," see Hasselberg, pp. 2350-2351; Lenin, passim; Marx and Engels, passim.
6. *Confederate Veteran*, July 1901, Vol. 9, No. 7, p. 318.
7. Long and Long, p. 602.
8. I have written dozens of books on these topics. See the Bibliography.
9. For a detailed discussion of this topic, see my book: *Lincoln's War: The Real Cause, the Real Winner, the Real Loser*.
10. For example, though slavery was constitutionally legal nationwide at the time, Lincoln (whose administration and armies were full of radical Liberals and socialists) made the following ominous statement on June 16, 1858, suggesting that he was willing to use warfare to override the Constitution: "I believe this government cannot endure, permanently half slave and half free. . . It will become all one thing or all the other." The South viewed this as a threat, and it was, as Lincoln proved on April 15, 1861, when he called for 75,000 troops to illegally invade the South. For a detailed discussion of these and other related topics, see my book: *Abraham Lincoln: The Southern View*.
11. For a detailed discussion of this topic, see my book: *All We Ask is to be Let Alone: The Southern Secession Fact Book*.
12. Seabrook, EOTBOF, s.v. "Battle of Franklin."
13. Seabrook, EOTBOF, s.v. "Battle of Nasvhille."
14. Field, p. 214.
15. Suspiciously, some 50 years after the War a Union veteran named J. D. Remington came forward claiming to be a Yankee spy responsible for Hood's "failure at Spring Hill." According to his account, Remington, masquerading as a Confederate captain, prevented Hood from ordering an attack on Schofield's troops by lying about their size. Based on Remington's greatly exaggerated numbers, Hood then decided to withhold battle until Franklin (when Lee's Corps would catch up with him) rather than risk tremendous loss at Spring Hill. In carefully studying Remington's story I have concluded, along with a number of Confederate veterans in the early 1900s, that it is a fiction from end to end, filled with holes, contradictions, improbabilities, and impossibilities. In 1914 J. P. Young, as just one example, a soldier who served with Forrest, rightly called it a "pipe dream." For this reason I have not included it in this book.
16. Hood, pp. 281-291. Note: The title of this entry is my own.
17. See Provine, p. 77.
18. Original note: "This charge, though omitted in his report by General Bradley, was mentioned both by General Wagner and General Forrest, and is affirmed by General Chalmers, who led it."
19. Original note: "It was this regiment probably, as it lay in some rail pen defenses after being driven back near Bradley's position in the edge of the woods in his front, that was charged by Chalmers with his escort and Wilson's Regiment (mounted) and that so sharply repulsed him. This was just before Cleburne's attack on Bradley's right."
20. Original note: "Cheatham's narrative and those of Generals Bate, Brown, Lowrey, and others, published in the *Courier-Journal* of Louisville, Ky., December 4, 1881, are hereinafter quoted from as required in this narrative."
21. Original note: "General Cleburne and General Forrest both rode in the rear of Govan's Brigade, in the center of the line, and, in company with General Govan during this charge, with drawn swords personally directed the movement."
22. Original note: "These were composed of Battery A, $1^{st}$ Ohio Light Artillery, four guns; Battery G, $1^{st}$ Ohio Light Artillery, six guns; Battery B, Pennsylvania Veteran Volunteers, four guns; and Battery M, $4^{th}$ United States Artillery, four guns."
23. Original note: "This attack on the $36^{th}$ Illinois and section of Battery B is described mostly in reports of Federal officers. It is not mentioned by Confederate writers who describe the battle. The section of artillery is referred to by the latter, but not the regiment."
24. Original note: "It was General Schofield who had authorized General Stanley 'in his discretion to burn the wagon train' and Gen. T. J. Wood who 'strongly advised' him to exercise this discretion." Statement of Capt. Shellenbarger.
25. *Confederate Veteran*, January 1908, Vol. 16, No. 1, pp. 29-41.
26. McMurray, pp. 329-338.
27. *Confederate Veteran*, July 1904, Vol. 12, No. 7, p. 338. Note: The title of this entry is my own.

28. *Confederate Veteran*, July 1904, Vol. 12, No. 7, p. 350. Of Garrard's words, Sumner A. Cunningham later wrote: "While the worst blunder of the war occurred at Spring Hill . . . [I do] not concur in the censure of any officer, unless it be Gen. Hood himself." Note: The title of this entry is my own.
29. *Confederate Veteran*, March 1907, Vol. 15, No. 3, p. 124.
30. *Confederate Veteran*, November 1907, Vol. 15, No. 11, p. 508. Note: The title of this entry is my own.
31. *Confederate Veteran*, April 1908, Vol. 16, No. 4, p. 187.
32. *Confederate Veteran*, June 1908, Vol. 16, No. 6, pp. 257-258. Note: The title of this entry is my own.
33. *Confederate Veteran*, September 1908, Vol. 16, No. 9, pp. 462-463. Note: The title of this entry is my own.
34. *Confederate Veteran*, January 1909, Vol. 17, No. 1, p. 32. Note: The title of this entry is my own.
35. *Confederate Veteran*, October 1908, Vol. 16, No. 10, p. 595. Note: The title of this entry is my own.
36. *Confederate Veteran*, August 1909, Vol. 17, No. 8, p. 383. Note: The title of this entry is my own.
37. *Confederate Veteran*, August 1909, Vol. 17, No. 8, p. 397. Note: The title of this entry is my own.
38. *Confederate Veteran*, January 1910, Vol. 18, No. 1, pp. 17-18. Note: The title of this entry is my own.
39. *Confederate Veteran*, July 1910, Vol. 18, No. 7, p. 326. Note: The title of this entry is my own.
40. Riley, p. 336. Note: The title of this entry is my own.
41. *Confederate Veteran*, September 1910, Vol. 18, No. 9, p. 416. Note: The title of this entry is my own.
42. *Confederate Veteran*, September 1910, Vol. 18, No. 9, p. 426.
43. Seabrook, ARB (2015 paperback edition), pp. 401-402.
44. *Confederate Veteran*, January 1914, Vol. 22, No. 1, pp. 14-15. Note: The title of this entry is my own.
45. "Mrs. Peters" was none other than the famous Southern belle Jessie McKissack Peters, wife of Dr. George B. Peters. Her romantic affair with Confederate General Earl Van Dorn earned her an unenviable Tennessee-wide reputation. On discovering the illicit relationship, Dr. Peters rode to the Martin Cheairs home (today known as "Ferguson Hall"), Van Dorn's headquarters in Spring Hill, and assassinated him. Forrest was later given Van Dorn's command of the cavalry on the left wing of the Army of Tennessee. Jessie's sister was Susan P. McKissack, who married Confederate Major Nathaniel F. Cheairs, my 4th cousin and the founder and builder of Rippavilla. See Seabrook, *The McGavocks of Carnton Plantation*, p. 355, passim.
46. *Confederate Veteran*, January 1914, Vol. 22, No. 1, p. 15. Note: The title of this entry is my own.
47. ORA, Ser. 1, Vol. 45, Pt. 2, p. 732. Harris was governor of Tennessee at the start of the War and remained so until Nashville was taken over by Yankees in 1862. He then joined the Confederate military, volunteering as an aide-de-camp to numerous officers, including Gen. John Bell Hood—which is why he was at the Battle of Spring Hill. Note: The title of this entry is my own.
48. *Confederate Veteran*, January 1914, Vol. 22, No. 1, p. 14. Note: The title of this entry is my own.
49. Cox, TMTTS, pp. 73-80. Original note: "A paper read in December, 1881, before a society of Southern officers at Louisville, Ky., by General Cheatham, contains a very full array of the evidence which sustains the above view." Note: The title of this entry is my own.
50. Shellenberger, pp. 20-26. Note: The title of this entry is my own.
51. *Confederate Veteran*, April 1903, Vol. 11, No. 4, pp. 165-166. Note: The title of this entry is my own.
52. *Confederate Veteran*, April 1903, Vol. 11, No. 4, pp. 167-168. Note: The title of this entry is my own.
53. *Confederate Veteran*, July 1904, Vol. 12, No. 7, p. 346. Note: The title of this entry is my own.
54. *Confederate Veteran*, December 1905, Vol. 13, No. 12, pp. 563, 564. Note: The title of this entry is my own.
55. *Confederate Veteran*, October 1908, Vol. 16, No. 10, p. 554. Note: The title of this entry is my own.
56. Field, pp. 216-220. Note: The title of this entry is my own.
57. Some modern historians state that the number of Confederate troops present was around 12,000. But this contradicts the accounts of eyewitnesses like Confederate officer J. P. Young. *Vide supra*, p. 31.
58. Seabrook, TMOCP, p. 346.
59. For more on these topics, see my book: *Everything You Were Taught About the Civil War is Wrong, Ask a Southerner!*
60. For more on these topics, see my book: *Everything You Were Taught About American Slavery is Wrong, Ask a Southerner!*
61. For more on these topics, see my book: *All We Ask is to be Let Alone: The Southern Secession Fact Book*.
62. For more on the topic of the realties behind the American "Civil War," see my book: *Lincoln's War: The Real Cause, the Real Winner, the Real Loser*.
63. For more on the topic of Confederate monuments, see my book: *Confederate Monuments: Why Every American Should Honor Confederate Soldiers and Their Memorials*.
64. *Confederate Veteran*, January 1910, Vol. 18, No. 1, p. 20.

# BIBLIOGRAPHY

## And Suggested Reading

Allardice, Bruce S. *Confederate Colonels: A Biographical Register*. Columbia, MO: University of Missouri Press, 2008.
Benson, Al, Jr., and Walter Donald Kennedy. *Lincoln's Marxists*. Gretna, LA: Pelican, 2011.
Boyd, James P. *Parties, Problems, and Leaders of 1896: An Impartial Presentation of Living National Questions*. Chicago, IL: Publishers' Union, 1896.
Brock, Robert Alonzo (ed.). *Southern Historical Society Papers*. 52 vols. Richmond, VA: Southern Historical Society, 1876-1943.
Browder, Earl. *Lincoln and the Communists*. New York, NY: Workers Library Publishers, Inc., 1936.
Bryan, William Jennings. *The First Battle: A Story of the Campaign of 1896*. Chicago, IL: W. B. Conkey Co., 1896.
Burns, James MacGregor. *The Vineyard of Liberty*. New York, NY: Alfred A. Knopf, 1982.
Christian, George Llewellyn. *Abraham Lincoln: An Address Delivered Before R. E. Lee Camp, No. 1 Confederate Veterans at Richmond, VA, October 29, 1909*. Richmond, VA: L. H. Jenkins, 1909.
———. *A Capitol Disaster: A Chapter of Reconstruction in Virginia*. Richmond, VA: self-published, 1915.
———. *Confederate Memories and Experiences*. Richmond, VA: self-published, 1915.
Cist, Henry M., W. F. Goodspeed, and H. A. Kelly (eds.). *Reunion of the Society of the Army of the Cumberland*, Vol. 16. Cincinnati, OH: Robert Clark and Co., 1885.
Clark, Charles T. *Opdycke Tigers 125th O.V.I.: A History of the Regiment and the Campaigns and Battles of the Army of the Cumberland*. Columbus, OH: Spahr and Glenn, 1895.
*Confederate Veteran* (Sumner A. Cunningham, ed.). 40 vols. Nashville, TN: Confederate Veteran, 1893-1932.
Cox, Jacob Dolson. *The March to the Sea: Franklin and Nashville* (Vol. 10). New York, NY: Charles Scribner's Sons, 1882.
———. *The Battle of Franklin, Tennessee, November 30, 1864: A Monograph*. New York, NY: Charles Scribner's Sons, 1897.
Davis, Jefferson. *The Rise and Fall of the Confederate Government*. 2 vols. New York, NY: D. Appleton and Co., 1881.
Evans, Clement Anselm (ed.). *Confederate Military History*. 12 vols. Atlanta, GA: Confederate Publishing Co., 1899.
Field, Henry Martyn. *Bright Skies and Dark Shadows*. New York, NY: Charles Scribner's Sons, 1890.
Franklin, John Hope. *Reconstruction After the Civil War*. Chicago, IL: University of Chicago Press, 1961.
Hasselberg, P. D. (ed.). *Parliamentary Debates: First Session, Fortieth Parliament, 1982, House of Representatives* (Vol. 445). Wellington, New Zealand: Government Printer, 1982.
Hay, Thomas Robson. *Hood's Tennessee Campaign*. New York, NY: W. Neale, 1929.
Hood, John Bell. *Advance and Retreat: Personal Experiences in the United States and Confederate States Armies*. New Orleans, LA: G. T. Beauregard, 1880.
Johnson, Robert Underwood, and Clarence Clough Buel (eds.). *Battles and Leaders of the Civil War*. 4 vols. New York, NY: The Century Co., 1884-1888.
Johnstone, Huger William. *Truth of War Conspiracy, 1861*. Idylwild, GA: H. W. Johnstone, 1921.
Jones, John William. *The Davis Memorial Volume; Or Our Dead President, Jefferson Davis and the World's Tribute to His Memory*. Richmond, VA: B. F. Johnson, 1889.
La Bree, Ben (ed.). *The Confederate Soldier in the Civil War, 1861-1865*. Louisville, KY: Prentice Press, 1897.
Lenin, Vladimir. *"Left Wing" Communism: An Infantile Disorder*. Detroit, MI: The Marxian Educational Society, 1921.

Livermore, Thomas L. *Numbers and Losses in the Civil War in America, 1861-65.* 1900. Carlisle, PA: John Kallmann, 1996 ed.
Long, Everette Beach, and Barbara Long. *The Civil War Day by Day: An Almanac 1861-1865.* 1971. Cambridge, MA: Da Capo, 1985 ed.
Magliocca, Gerard N. *The Tragedy of William Jennings Bryan: Constitutional Law and the Politics of Backlash.* New Haven, CT: Yale University Press, 2011.
Marx, Karl, and Frederick Engels. *Manifesto of the Communist Party.* Chicago, IL: Charles H. Kerr and Co., 1906.
McCarty, Burke (ed.). *Little Sermons in Socialism by Abraham Lincoln.* Chicago, IL: The Chicago Daily Socialist, 1910.
McPherson, James M. *Abraham Lincoln and the Second American Revolution.* New York, NY: Oxford University Press, 1991.
Meriwether, Elizabeth Avery (pseudonym, "George Edmonds"). *Facts and Falsehoods Concerning the War on the South, 1861-1865.* Memphis, TN: A. R. Taylor and Co., 1904.
Miller, Francis Trevelyan, and Robert S. Lanier (eds.). *The Photographic History of the Civil War.* 10 vols. New York, NY: The Review of Reviews Co., 1911.
*Minutes of the Eighth Annual Meeting and Reunion of the United Confederate Veterans,* Atlanta, GA, July 20-23, 1898. New Orleans, LA: United Confederate Veterans, 1907.
*Minutes of the Ninth Annual Meeting and Reunion of the United Confederate Veterans,* Charleston, SC, May 10-13, 1899. New Orleans, LA: United Confederate Veterans, 1907.
*Minutes of the Twelfth Annual Meeting and Reunion of the United Confederate Veterans,* Dallas, TX, April 22-25, 1902. New Orleans, LA: United Confederate Veterans, 1907.
Muzzey, David Saville. *The United States of America: Vol. 1, To the Civil War.* Boston, MA: Ginn and Co., 1922.
———. *The American Adventure: Vol. 2, From the Civil War.* 1924. New York, NY: Harper and Brothers, 1927 ed.
Newlin, W. H., D. F. Lawler, and J. W. Sherrick (eds.). *A History of the Seventy-third Regiment of Illinois Infantry Volunteers.* Illinois: Regimental Reunion Association of Survivors of the 73rd Illinois Infantry Volunteers.
Nicolay, John G., and John Hay (eds.). *Abraham Lincoln: A History.* 10 vols. New York, NY: The Century Co., 1890.
———. *Complete Works of Abraham Lincoln.* 12 vols. 1894. New York, NY: Francis D. Tandy Co., 1905 ed.
———. *Abraham Lincoln: Complete Works.* 12 vols. 1894. New York, NY: The Century Co., 1907 ed.
ORA (full title: *The War of the Rebellion: A Compilation of the Official Records of the Union and Confederate Armies*). 70 vols. Washington, DC: Government Printing Office, 1880.
ORN (full title: *Official Records of the Union and Confederate Navies in the War of the Rebellion*). 30 vols. Washington, DC: Government Printing Office, 1894.
Pollard, Edward Alfred. *The Lost Cause.* New York, NY: E. B. Treat and Co., 1867.
Provine, William A. (ed.). *Tennessee Historical Magazine,* April 1921, Vol. 7, No. 1. Nashville, TN: Tennessee Historical Society, 1921.
Richardson, John Anderson. *Richardson's Defense of the South.* Atlanta, GA: A. B. Caldwell, 1914.
Riley, Franklin L. (ed.). *Publications of the Mississippi Historical Society,* Vols. 10, 11. University, MS: Mississippi Historical Society, 1910.
Rogers, William P. *The Three Secession Movements in the United States: Samuel J. Tilden, the Democratic Candidate for Presidency; the Advisor, Aider and Abettor of the Great Secession Movement of 1860; and One of the Authors of the Infamous Resolution of 1864; His Claims as a Statesman and Reformer Considered.* Boston, MA: John Wilson and Son, 1876.
Rove, Karl. *The Triumph of William McKinley: Why the Election of 1896 Still Matters.* New York, NY: Simon and Schuster, 2015.
Rutherford, Mildred Lewis. *Truths of History: A Fair, Unbiased, Impartial, Unprejudiced and Conscientious Study of History.* Athens, GA: n.p., 1920.
Seabrook, Lochlainn. *Carnton Plantation Ghost Stories: True Tales of the Unexplained from Tennessee's*

———. *Most Haunted Civil War House!* 2005. Franklin, TN, 2016 ed.
———. *Nathan Bedford Forrest: Southern Hero, American Patriot.* 2007. Franklin, TN, 2010 ed.
———. *Abraham Lincoln: The Southern View.* 2007. Franklin, TN: Sea Raven Press, 2013 ed.
———. *The McGavocks of Carnton Plantation: A Southern History - Celebrating One of Dixie's Most Noble Confederate Families and Their Tennessee Home.* 2008. Franklin, TN, 2011ed.
———. *A Rebel Born: A Defense of Nathan Bedford Forrest.* 2010. Franklin, TN: Sea Raven Press, 2011 ed.
———. *A Rebel Born: The Screenplay* (for the film). 2011. Franklin, TN: Sea Raven Press.
———. *Everything You Were Taught About the Civil War is Wrong, Ask a Southerner!* 2010. Franklin, TN: Sea Raven Press, revised 2014 ed.
———. *The Quotable Jefferson Davis: Selections From the Writings and Speeches of the Confederacy's First President.* Franklin, TN: Sea Raven Press, 2011.
———. *The Quotable Robert E. Lee: Selections From the Writings and Speeches of the South's Most Beloved Civil War General.* Franklin, TN: Sea Raven Press, 2011 Sesquicentennial Civil War Edition.
———. *Lincolnology: The Real Abraham Lincoln Revealed In His Own Words.* Franklin, TN: Sea Raven Press, 2011.
———. *The Unquotable Abraham Lincoln: The President's Quotes They Don't Want You To Know!* Franklin, TN: Sea Raven Press, 2011.
———. *Honest Jeff and Dishonest Abe: A Southern Children's Guide to the Civil War.* Franklin, TN: Sea Raven Press, 2012.
———. *Encyclopedia of the Battle of Franklin - A Comprehensive Guide to the Conflict that Changed the Civil War.* Franklin, TN: Sea Raven Press, 2012.
———. *The Quotable Nathan Bedford Forrest: Selections From the Writings and Speeches of the Confederacy's Most Brilliant Cavalryman.* Spring Hill, TN: Sea Raven Press, 2012.
———. *Forrest! 99 Reasons to Love Nathan Bedford Forrest.* Spring Hill, TN: Sea Raven Press, 2012.
———. *Give 'Em Hell Boys! The Complete Military Correspondence of Nathan Bedford Forrest.* Spring Hill, TN: Sea Raven Press, 2012.
———. *The Constitution of the Confederate States of America Explained: A Clause-by-Clause Study of the South's Magna Carta.* Spring Hill, TN: Sea Raven Press, 2012 Sesquicentennial Civil War Edition.
———. *The Great Impersonator: 99 Reasons to Dislike Abraham Lincoln.* Spring Hill, TN: Sea Raven Press, 2012.
———. *The Old Rebel: Robert E. Lee As He Was Seen By His Contemporaries.* Spring Hill, TN: Sea Raven Press, 2012 Sesquicentennial Civil War Edition.
———. *The Quotable Stonewall Jackson: Selections From the Writings and Speeches of the South's Most Famous General.* Spring Hill, TN: Sea Raven Press, 2012 Sesquicentennial Civil War Edition.
———. *Saddle, Sword, and Gun: A Biography of Nathan Bedford Forrest for Teens.* Spring Hill, TN: Sea Raven Press, 2013.
———. *The Alexander H. Stephens Reader: Excerpts From the Works of a Confederate Founding Father.* Spring Hill, TN: Sea Raven Press, 2013.
———. *The Quotable Alexander H. Stephens: Selections From the Writings and Speeches of the Confederacy's First Vice President.* Spring Hill, TN: Sea Raven Press, 2013 Sesquicentennial Civil War Edition.
———. *Give This Book to a Yankee! A Southern Guide to the Civil War for Northerners.* Spring Hill, TN: Sea Raven Press, 2014.
———. *The Articles of Confederation Explained: A Clause-by-Clause Study of America's First Constitution.* Spring Hill, TN: Sea Raven Press, 2014.
———. *Confederate Blood and Treasure: An Interview With Lochlainn Seabrook.* Spring Hill, TN: Sea Raven Press, 2015.
———. *Nathan Bedford Forrest and the Battle of Fort Pillow: Yankee Myth, Confederate Fact.* Spring Hill, TN: Sea Raven Press, 2015.
———. *Everything You Were Taught About American Slavery War is Wrong, Ask a Southerner!* Spring Hill, TN: Sea Raven Press, 2015.
———. *Confederacy 101: Amazing Facts You Never Knew About America's Oldest Political Tradition.* Spring

Hill, TN: Sea Raven Press, 2015.
——. *The Great Yankee Coverup: What the North Doesn't Want You to Know About Lincoln's War!* Spring Hill, TN: Sea Raven Press, 2015.
——. *Slavery 101: Amazing Facts You Never Knew About America's "Peculiar Institution."* Spring Hill, TN: Sea Raven Press, 2015.
——. *Confederate Flag Facts: What Every American Should Know About Dixie's Southern Cross.* Spring Hill, TN: Sea Raven Press, 2016.
——. *Nathan Bedford Forrest and the Ku Klux Klan: Yankee Myth, Confederate Fact.* Spring Hill, TN: Sea Raven Press, 2016.
——. *Seabrook's Bible Dictionary of Traditional and Mystical Christian Doctrines.* Spring Hill, TN: Sea Raven Press, 2016.
——. *Everything You Were Taught About African-Americans and the Civil War is Wrong, Ask a Southerner!* Spring Hill, TN: Sea Raven Press, 2016.
——. *Nathan Bedford Forrest and African-Americans: Yankee Myth, Confederate Fact.* Spring Hill, TN: Sea Raven Press, 2016.
——. *Women in Gray: A Tribute to the Ladies Who Supported the Southern Confederacy.* Spring Hill, TN: Sea Raven Press, 2016.
——. *Lincoln's War: The Real Cause, the Real Winner, the Real Loser.* Spring Hill, TN: Sea Raven Press, 2016.
——. *The Unholy Crusade: Lincoln's Legacy of Destruction in the American South.* Spring Hill, TN: Sea Raven Press, 2017.
——. *Abraham Lincoln Was a Liberal, Jefferson Davis Was a Conservative: The Missing Key to Understanding the American Civil War.* Spring Hill, TN: Sea Raven Press, 2017.
——. *All We Ask is to be Let Alone: The Southern Secession Fact Book.* Spring Hill, TN: Sea Raven Press, 2017.
——. *The Ultimate Civil War Quiz Book: How Much Do You Really Know About America's Most Misunderstood Conflict?* Spring Hill, TN: Sea Raven Press, 2017.
——. *Rise Up and Call Them Blessed: Victorian Tributes to the Confederate Soldier, 1861-1901.* Spring Hill, TN: Sea Raven Press, 2017.
——. *Victorian Confederate Poetry: The Southern Cause in Verse, 1861-1901.* Spring Hill, TN: Sea Raven Press, 2018.
——. *Confederate Monuments: Why Every American Should Honor Confederate Soldiers and Their Memorials.* Spring Hill, TN: Sea Raven Press, 2018.
——. *The God of War: Nathan Bedford Forrest as He Was Seen by His Contemporaries.* Spring Hill, TN: Sea Raven Press, 2018.
Shellenberger, John K. *The Battle of Spring Hill, Tennessee.* 1907. Cleveland, OH: Arthur H. Clark Co., 1913 ed.
Steel, Samuel Augustus. *The South Was Right.* Columbia, SC: R. L. Bryan Co., 1914.
Stephens, Alexander Hamilton. *Speech of Mr. Stephens, of Georgia, on the War and Taxation.* Washington, D.C.: J & G. Gideon, 1848.
——. *A Constitutional View of the Late War Between the States; Its Causes, Character, Conduct and Results.* 2 vols. Philadelphia, PA: National Publishing, Co., 1870.
——. *Recollections of Alexander H. Stephens: His Diary Kept When a Prisoner at Fort Warren, Boston Harbour, 1865.* New York, NY: Doubleday, Page, and Co., 1910.
Stewart, James Jr. (ed.). *The Union Army.* 8 vols. Madison, WI: Federal Publishing Co., 1908.
Sword, Wiley. *Embrace an Angry Wind, The Confederacy's Last Hurrah: Spring Hill, Franklin, and Nashville.* Columbus, OH: The General's Books, 1994.
Thompson, Holland. *The New South: A Chronicle of Social and Industrial Evolution.* New Haven, CT: Yale University Press, 1920.
Warner, Ezra J. *Generals in Gray: Lives of the Confederate Commanders.* 1959. Baton Rouge, LA: Louisiana State University Press, 1989 ed.
——. *Generals in Blue: Lives of the Union Commanders.* 1964. Baton Rouge, LA: Louisiana State University Press, 2006 ed.
Woods, Thomas E., Jr. *The Politically Incorrect Guide to American History.* Washington, D.C.: Regnery, 2004.

# MEET THE AUTHOR

"DEMANDING THAT THE PATRIOTIC SOUTH STOP HONORING HER CONFEDERATE ANCESTORS IS LIKE DEMANDING THE SUN NOT TO SHINE." — COLONEL LOCHLAINN SEABROOK

**OCHLAINN SEABROOK**, a neo-Victorian and world acclaimed man of letters, is a Kentucky Colonel and the winner of the prestigious Jefferson Davis Historical Gold Medal for his "masterpiece," *A Rebel Born: A Defense of Nathan Bedford Forrest*. A classic littérateur and an unreconstructed Southern historian, he is an award-winning author, "Civil War" scholar, Confederate culture expert, Bible authority, the leading popularizer of American Civil War history, and a traditional Southern Agrarian of Scottish, English, Irish, Dutch, Welsh, German, and Italian extraction.

Above, Colonel Lochlainn Seabrook, "the voice of the traditional South," award-winning Civil War scholar and unreconstructed Southern historian. America's most popular and prolific pro-South author, his many books have introduced hundreds of thousands to the truth about the War for Southern Independence. He coined the phrase "South-shaming" and holds the world record for writing the most books on Nathan Bedford Forrest.

A child prodigy, Seabrook is today a true Renaissance Man whose occupational titles also include encyclopedist, lexicographer, musician, artist, graphic designer, genealogist, photographer, and award-winning poet. Also a songwriter and a screenwriter, he has a 40 year background in historical nonfiction writing and is a member of the Sons of Confederate Veterans, the Civil War Trust, and the National Grange.

Known to his many fans as the "voice of the traditional South," due to similarities in their writing styles, ideas, and literary works, Seabrook is also often referred to as the "new Shelby Foote," the "Southern Joseph Campbell," and the "American Robert Graves" (his English cousin). Seabrook coined the terms "South-shaming" and "Lincolnian liberalism," and holds the world's record for writing the most books on Nathan Bedford Forrest. In addition, Seabrook is the first Civil War scholar to connect the early American nickname for the U.S., "The Confederate States of America," with the Southern Confederacy that arose eight decades later, and the first to note that in 1860 the party platforms of the two major political parties were the opposite of what they are today (Victorian Democrats were Conservatives, Victorian Republicans were Liberals).

The son of a Kentucky trainman and the grandson of Appalachian coal-mining and farming families, Seabrook is a seventh-generation Kentuckian whose European ancestors came from Virginia, North Carolina, and Tennessee, settling in the Bluegrass State in the early 1700s, thereafter spreading into West Virginia, the Midwest, and finally the West.

Seabrook is co-chair of the Jent/Gent Family Committee (Kentucky), founder and director of the Blakeney Family Tree Project, and a board member of the Friends of Colonel Benjamin E. Caudill. His literary works have been endorsed by leading authorities, museum curators, award-winning historians, bestselling authors, celebrities, filmmakers, noted scientists, well regarded educators, TV show hosts and producers, renowned military artists, esteemed Southern organizations, and distinguished academicians from around the world.

Seabrook has authored over 50 popular adult books on the American Civil War, American and international slavery, the U.S. Confederacy (1781), the Southern Confederacy (1861), religion, theology, thealogy, Jesus, the Bible, the Apocrypha, the Law of Attraction, alternative health, spirituality, ghost stories, the paranormal, ufology, social issues, and cross-cultural studies of the family and marriage. His Confederate biographies, pro-South studies, Victorian Southern literature titles, genealogical monographs, family histories, military encyclopedias, self-help guides, and etymological dictionaries have received wide acclaim.

Seabrook's eight children's books include a Southern guide to the "Civil War," a biography of Nathan Bedford Forrest, a dictionary of religion and myth, a rewriting of the King Arthur legend (which reinstates the original pre-Christian motifs), two bedtime stories for preschoolers, a naturalist's guidebook to owls, a worldwide look at the family, and an examination of the Near-Death Experience.

Of blue-blooded Southern stock through his Kentucky, Tennessee, Virginia, North Carolina and West Virginia ancestors, he is a direct descendant of European royalty via his 6$^{th}$ great-grandfather, the Earl of Oxford, after which London's famous Harley Street is named. Among his celebrated male Celtic ancestors is Robert the Bruce, King of Scotland, Seabrook's 22$^{nd}$ great-grandfather. The 21$^{st}$ great-grandson of Edward I "Longshanks" Plantagenet), King of England, Seabrook is a 17$^{th}$-generation Southerner through his descent from the colonists of Jamestown, Virginia (1607).

The 2$^{nd}$, 3$^{rd}$, and 4$^{th}$ great-grandson of dozens of Confederate soldiers, one of his closest connections to Lincoln's War is through his 3$^{rd}$ great-grandfather, Elias Jent Sr., who fought for the Confederacy in the Thirteenth Cavalry Kentucky under Seabrook's 2$^{nd}$ cousin, Colonel Benjamin E. Caudill. The Thirteenth, also known as "Caudill's Army," fought in numerous conflicts, including the Battles of Saltville, Gladsville, Mill Cliff, Poor Fork, Whitesburg, and Leatherwood.

(Photo © Lochlainn Seabrook)

Seabrook is a direct descendant of the families of Alexander H. Stephens, John Singleton Mosby, William Giles Harding, and Edmund Winchester Rucker, and is related to the following Confederates and other 18$^{th}$- and 19$^{th}$-Century luminaries: Robert E. Lee, Stephen Dill Lee, Stonewall Jackson, Nathan Bedford Forrest, James Longstreet, John Hunt Morgan, Jeb Stuart, Pierre G. T. Beauregard (approved the Confederate Battle Flag design), George W. Gordon, John Bell Hood, Alexander Peter Stewart, Arthur M. Manigault, Joseph Manigault, Charles Scott Venable, Thornton A. Washington, John A. Washington, Abraham Buford, Edmund W. Pettus, Theodrick "Tod" Carter, John B. Womack, John H. Winder, Gideon J. Pillow, States Rights Gist, Henry R. Jackson, John Lawton Seabrook, John C. Breckinridge, Leonidas Polk, Zachary Taylor, Sarah Knox Taylor (first wife of Jefferson Davis), Richard Taylor, Davy Crockett, Daniel Boone, Meriwether Lewis (of the Lewis and Clark Expedition) Andrew Jackson, James K. Polk, Abram Poindexter Maury (founder of Franklin,

TN), Zebulon Baird Vance, Thomas Jefferson, Edmund Jennings Randolph, George Wythe Randolph (grandson of Jefferson), Felix K. Zollicoffer, Fitzhugh Lee, Nathaniel F. Cheairs, Jesse James, Frank James, Robert Brank Vance, Charles Sidney Winder, John W. McGavock, Caroline E. (Winder) McGavock, David Harding McGavock, Lysander McGavock, James Randal McGavock, Randal William McGavock, Francis McGavock, Emily McGavock, William Henry F. Lee, Lucius E. Polk, Minor Meriwether (husband of noted pro-South author Elizabeth Avery Meriwether), Ellen Bourne Tynes (wife of Forrest's chief of artillery, Captain John W. Morton), South Carolina Senators Preston Smith Brooks and Andrew Pickens Butler, and famed South Carolina diarist Mary Chesnut.

Seabrook's modern day cousins include: Patrick J. Buchanan (conservative author), Cindy Crawford (model), Shelby Lee Adams (Letcher Co., Kentucky, photographer), Bertram Thomas Combs (Kentucky's 50$^{th}$ governor), Edith Bolling (second wife of President Woodrow Wilson), and actors Andy Griffith, Riley Keough, George C. Scott, Robert Duvall, Reese Witherspoon, Lee Marvin, Rebecca Gayheart, and Tom Cruise.

Seabrook's screenplay, *A Rebel Born*, based on his book of the same name, has been signed with acclaimed filmmaker Christopher Forbes (of Forbes Film). Set for release as a full-length feature film, it is in pre-production, awaiting the necessary funding. This will be the first movie ever made of Nathan Bedford Forrest's life story, and as a historically accurate project written from the Southern perspective, is destined to be one of the most talked about Civil War films of all time.

Born with music in his blood, Seabrook is an award-winning, multi-genre, BMI-Nashville songwriter and lyricist who has composed some 3,000 songs (250 albums), and whose original music has been heard in film (*A Rebel Born, Cowgirls 'n Angels, Confederate Cavalry, Billy the Kid: Showdown in Lincoln County, Vengeance Without Mercy, Last Step, County Line, The Mark*) and on TV and radio worldwide. A musician, producer, multi-instrumentalist, and renown performer—whose keyboard work has been variously compared to pianists from Hargus Robbins and Vince Guaraldi to Elton John and Leonard Bernstein—Seabrook has opened for groups such as the Earl Scruggs Review, Ted Nugent, and Bob Seger, and has performed privately for such public figures as President Ronald Reagan, Burt Reynolds, Loni Anderson, and Senator Edward W. Brooke. Seabrook's cousins in the music business include: Johnny Cash, Elvis Presley, Lisa Marie Presley, Billy Ray and Miley Cyrus, Patty Loveless, Tim McGraw, Lee Ann Womack, Dolly Parton, Pat Boone, Naomi, Wynonna, and Ashley Judd, Ricky Skaggs, the Sunshine Sisters, Martha Carson, and Chet Atkins.

Seabrook lives with his wife and family in historic Middle Tennessee, the heart of Forrest country and the Confederacy, where his conservative Southern ancestors fought valiantly against Liberal Lincoln and the progressive North in defense of Jeffersonianism, constitutional government, and personal liberty.

**LochlainnSeabrook.com**

If you enjoyed this book you will be interested in Colonel Seabrook's other popular related titles:

- ENCYCLOPEDIA OF THE BATTLE OF FRANKLIN
- THE MCGAVOCKS OF CARNTON PLANTATION: A SOUTHERN HISTORY
- CARNTON PLANTATION GHOST STORIES
- ABRAHAM LINCOLN WAS A LIBERAL, JEFFERSON DAVIS WAS A CONSERVATIVE
- EVERYTHING YOU WERE TAUGHT ABOUT THE CIVIL WAR IS WRONG, ASK A SOUTHERNER!
- THE ULTIMATE CIVIL WAR QUIZ BOOK

*Available from Sea Raven Press and wherever fine books are sold*

ALL OF OUR BOOK COVERS ARE AVAILABLE AS 11" X 17" POSTERS, SUITABLE FOR FRAMING

# SeaRavenPress.com • NathanBedfordForrestBooks.com

www.ingramcontent.com/pod-product-compliance
Lightning Source LLC
LaVergne TN
LVHW041255080426
835510LV00009B/745